HIP TO
STITCH

HIP TO STITCH

20 Contemporary Projects Embellished with Thread

Melinda A. Barta

Project editor: Christine Townsend
Technical editor: Deanna Hall West
Illustrations: Ann Swanson
Photo styling: Ann Swanson
Photography: Joe Coca
Patterns: Dean Howes
Book design: Bren Frisch
Book production: Samantha L. Thaler
Copy editor: Stephen Beal
Proofreader and indexer: Nancy Arndt

Interweave Press, Inc.
201 East Fourth Street
Loveland, Colorado 80537-5655 USA
www.interweave.com

Printed in China by Everbest Printing Company

Library of Congress Cataloging-in-Publication Data

Barta, Melinda.
  Hip to stitch : 20 contemporary projects embellished with thread /
Melinda Barta.
      p. cm.
  Includes index.
  ISBN 1-931499-60-8
  1. Embroidery. 2. Fancy work. I. Title: Hip to stitch, twenty
contemporary projects embellished with thread. II. Title.
  TT770.B26 2005
  746.44--dc22
                                    2004018199

10 9 8 7 6 5 4 3 2 1

ACKNOWLEDGMENTS

This book is dedicated to my family—Ron, Jean, Carrie, and Rachel Barta, and Jason Waldron—with thanks for all the encouragement you provided every step of the way. ■ Special thanks to Jean Barta for helping stitch the pillows and tea towels and for her constant, steady guidance and support. ■ Thank you to everyone at Interweave Press who gave me the opportunity to write this book: Marilyn Murphy, Linda Ligon, Betsy Armstrong, and Linda Stark. ■ Many thanks as well to Ann Swanson, the editorial and production teams, and the support staff at Interweave Press for their talent, collaboration, and dedication; to Jeane Hutchins of *PieceWork* magazine for showing me how to execute some of my first projects; to fiber artists Tom Lundberg and Renie Breskin Adams for expanding my knowledge of embroidery and for all the fun and eye-opening classes and workshops; to Amy Clarke Moore for embellishing the beaded bag and sharing her wonderful tips on bead embroidery.

■ TABLE OF CONTENTS

1 Introduction

2 Basics

GETTING STARTED

16 Stitch Reference and Needle Storage Book

22 Korean-Inspired Thimbles

FOR KEEPS

28 Cuddle-Up Corduroy Coat

32 Trendy Hair Ties

38 Family Tree Textile Scrapbook

44 Cozy Crewel Mittens

FOR GIFTING

48 Rich Velvet Ribbons and a Radiant Beaded Bag

58 Antsy Baby Bib

64 Day Tripper Bag

70 Captured Butterfly Picture Frame

74 Free-Form Gift Tags, Cards, and Notebooks

78 Groovin' Guitar Pick Case

82 Map Your Favorite Escape

FOR THE HOME

86 Conversion Kitchen Towels

92 No-Tie Easy-Dry Cloths for Herbs and Flowers

96 Cocktail Party Apron

100 Which Came First Napkin Rings

104 Hybrid Grid Pillows

110 All-Mine Monogrammed Cases

116 Suppliers and Industry Resources

117 Index

Korean-inspired thimbles, page 22

STITCHES

Backstitch	20	Long-and-short satin stitch	20
Backstitch with beads	57	Modified surface satin stitch	31
Blanket stitch	89	One-sided fern stitch	63
Bookbinding stitch	19	Overcast stitch	21
Bound satin stitch	81	Running stitch	20
Braid edging stitch	98	Padded satin stitch over backstitch	112
Buttonhole stitch	71	Satin stitch	20
Chain stitch	21	Satin stitch over double running stitch	30
Colonial knots	35	Seed stitch	20
Coral stitch	84	Slip stitch	105
Couching	21	Split stitch	21
Couching with beads	57	Stem stitch	21
Detached buttonhole stitch	102	Straight stitch	20
Double running stitch	20	Surface satin stitch	31
French knots	21	Uneven slip stitch	90
Herringbone stitch	57	Vertical slip stitch	90
Knot stitch edging	41	Whipped backstitch	89
Lattice pattern filling stitch	47	Whipped stem stitch	24
Lazy daisy stitch	95	Whipstitch	103
Long-and-short blanket stitch	89		

Groovin' guitar pick case, page 78

Which came first napkin rings, page 100

Rich velvet ribbons, page 48

TIPS AND TECHNIQUES

31 Avoiding Bulk on the Under-side of Your Fabric

53 Backing Your Embroideries: Making Reversible Ribbons

90 Basic Hems: Making Your Own Tea Towels

56 Bead Embroidery 101

30 Choosing Durable Stitches

85 Designing an Embroidered Map

113 Designing Your Own Font Suitable for Monograms

102 Detached Buttonhole Stitch and Shaping Techniques

62 Fabric Stamping 101

27 Hiding Knots and Thread Tails

19 How to Bind a Book

42 How to Sew a Pocket

80 Managing Couched Threads

36 Quick and Easy Hair-Tie Tote

68 Quilting Basics: Piecing and Quilt Tying

109 Sewing Machine Basics

67 Tips for Iron Transfers and Printing on Fabric

77 Understanding and Using Your Sewing Machine's Tension

46 Working with Wool Threads

73 Working with Silk and Wire

INTRODUCTION

Embroidery is all around us—it blooms on our grandmothers' handkerchiefs, winds over our clothing, and adds touches of color and personality to our homes. Why not embellish and create these items yourself? Stitching is fun, easy, meditative, and a great way to turn the ordinary into the unique. Your wallet needn't be significantly burdened, either: With just a needle, thread, and a bit of cloth, you have all the pieces needed to stitch a portable, inexpensive work of art that's all your own. New material isn't even necessary; you may find, like me, some of your favorite projects revamp vintage materials.

■ From *Hip to Stitch*, novice stitchers will learn the basics of embroidery through thirty-eight easy-to-follow stitch illustrations, nineteen playful hand-embroidered projects, and one contemporary machine-embroidered project; experienced stitchers will find inspiration for a fresh approach to embroidery. The projects, divided into four categories, are accessible, functional, and practical: **Getting Started** (projects that help teach you the basics and in turn fill your sewing kit); **For Keeps** (items you'll want for yourself); **For Gifting** (meaningful gifts that friends and family will love); and **For the Home** (projects that help make your house a home).

■ In the Basics section, you will find basic information on embroidery and supplies—so, if you are a beginner or need a quick brush up, go there first. I encourage you to make the projects as simple or ambitious as you like by experimenting with stitches, threads, and motif quantity and placement. All of the illustrations are for right-handed stitchers; mirror accordingly if you prefer to stitch with your left hand. ■ The first chapter presents twelve basic stitches in the format of a functional needle book; following chapters showcase one or two new stitches or stitch variations. Keep an eye out for the twenty Tips and Techniques sidebars for design, construction, and tricks-of-the-trade ideas. The basics of bookbinding, pocket construction, sewing, crewel work, bead embroidery, fabric stamping, reverse appliqué, patchwork piecing and quilt tying, photograph transfers, stumpwork, sewing machine maintenance, hemming, and monogram design are all described in these sections. ■ On the following pages, stitchers of all skill levels will find projects that speak to them and spark their imaginations. I hope you discover the same magic I do when I am holding a needle threaded with richly colored strands. Most importantly, have fun with these projects, get inspired, and enjoy the process of creating and completing handmade embroideries. Your world will be all the more colorful!

1

BASICS

Supplies and Tips to Help You Get Started

■ CHOOSING, PREPARING, AND LAUNDERING FABRICS AND THREADS

The most important aspect to consider when choosing fabric and threads for embroidery is their quality. High-quality fabric, whether new or vintage, and threads are worth the investment when you think about the time and attention you will give a project. I used quilter's cotton (high thread count, 100 percent cotton fabric) and 100 percent cotton or 100 percent silk embroidery thread for nearly all the projects in this book. Higher-quality cotton fabrics are more balanced than lower-quality cottons because their vertical (warp) and horizontal (weft) threads meet at a 90-degree angle. Fabrics that are not balanced are difficult to cut into perfect squares and may distort your embroidered motifs. Keep an open mind when looking for fabrics; I used a napkin and placemat to make the bag on page 54.

Prewashing fabrics will prevent any surprises that may arise when you wash your completed embroideries. Prewashing removes any sizing materials that may have been added during manufacturing, removes excess dye from richly colored fabrics, and preshrinks the material. Iron the washed fabric and lightly starch if you are working with thin fabrics or if you have difficulty removing all the wrinkles. If your iron does not release an adequate amount of steam, use a damp press cloth. It is best to always iron embroidered pieces face down on a white terry-cloth towel and use a thin, white cotton press cloth on the back of the fabric.

Keep in mind all the steps needed to complete a project when you choose the fabric and threads. For example, if you are required to back your fabric with interfacing and if the manufacturer requires you to use a hot iron during the fusing process, do not use heat-sensitive synthetic or silk fabrics. Also keep in mind the end use of the item: If it is going to be worn as everyday clothing, heavily used, or given to a child, choose fabrics like cotton and linen that are easy to launder. When you're choosing threads, remember that some threads, like silk, are dry-clean only.

Choose high-quality threads and fabric

2

Whenever possible, match the fiber content of your sewing thread and fabric—doing so will help prevent surprises with distortion and shrinkage caused by washing and will guarantee even wear of both the threads and fabric over time.

Balls of green and red thread

When you are finished stitching, it is a good idea to rinse the item in three or four changes of cold water to remove the lines left by water-soluble marking pens and, if applicable, any excess dye that may still be held in the threads. Omit this step if the embroidered item was made with silk or will never be washed or exposed to moisture (like the Captured Butterfly Picture Frame on page 70). It is always best to consult the manufacturer's directions when you're removing marking materials; most may be removed with a fabric eraser available at craft stores, a damp cloth, by machine washing, or with natural exposure to air.

If you need to remove faint pencil marks or dirt, gently wash the stitched fabric with mild soap. Roll wet embroidered items in a white terry-cloth towel and lightly squeeze to absorb the moisture; dry by pressing face down on a dry terry-cloth towel with a pressing cloth and the hottest iron the fabric and thread can withstand.

DMC and Anchor are the two most common manufacturers of 100 percent cotton six-strand embroidery thread. Both brands are offered in hundreds of colors and are suitable for all the projects in this book that call for six-strand 100 percent cotton thread. See the conversion chart on page 15 to select thread colors.

■ CUTTING FABRIC

A clear quilt ruler, self-healing cutting mat, and a rotary cutter (available with replacement blades) make cutting lines quick, easy, and accurate, and they keep your hands from getting tired using scissors. The best rulers are large enough for you to hold down with either the palm or all five fingers of the noncutting hand and are at least $1/8$ inch (3 mm) thick (I suggest starting with a ruler that is at least 12 × 6 inches [30.5 × 15.2 cm] and covered with fine black grid lines). Cutting mats designed for quilters will protect the work surface and last for years, if properly stored away from heat and direct sunlight. The term self-healing literally means that cuts in the mat will disappear over time.

To achieve the most accurate cuts, press fabric before cutting. If you are using lightweight and loosely woven fabrics that won't lie flat, lightly starch the fabric before cutting. Your cuts will also be more accurate if you start with at least one 90-degree angle. To square up the raw edges of a piece of fabric, sandwich the fabric between the mat and the clear ruler with a raw edge of the fabric sticking out from under the right side of the ruler (reverse if you are

Make accurate and time-saving cuts with a rotary cutter

3

left-handed). Make a vertical cut by rolling the rotary cutter alongside the ruler with the blade flush to the side of the ruler. Lift the ruler, align the trimmed edge with the bottom grid line on the mat, and lay the ruler on top of the fabric with one of the other raw edges of the fabric sticking out from under the right (or left) edge of the ruler and one of the horizontal grid lines on the ruler aligned with the previously cut edge. Trim along the ruler's edge with the rotary cutter to create a second straight edge and a 90-degree corner.

To make additional cuts, it is always best to line up the straight edges of the fabric with lines on the mat and to align the grid of the mat with the grid of the ruler. It is easiest to do so when the fabric you are trimming is smaller than the mat. This method of cutting is also ideal for trimming paper for scrapbooking and card making. Paper will dull the blade of your rotary cutter, so store two properly contained blades in your sewing basket and use one only for fabric and the other only for paper.

Have an assortment of scissors for different uses

If you prefer to use scissors instead of rotary cutters to make straight cuts, keep one pair for use with fabric only; paper will dull the blades. To prevent the edges of fabric from fraying, use pinking shears (shears with zigzag-edged blades). Both scissors and shears are appropriate for cutting fabric: Scissors have even-sized handles and shears have ergonomically designed, uneven-sized handles. Shears are generally heavier than scissors and have longer blades (an average of 4 inches [10.2 cm]). Embroidery scissors have small blades (an average of 2 inches [5.1 cm]) and sometimes have curved ends that prevent you from accidentally cutting fabric when you're trimming threads.

■ FUSIBLE INTERFACING AND FUSIBLE WEB

Both these nonwoven products are adhered to the back of fabric with an iron and are available in various weights. Interfacing, most commonly available in white, is used for stiffening and stabilizing the back of fabric; you'll find it in everyday shirt collars and cuffs. This material is fused to fabric before stitching and the manufacturer's directions usually require a damp press cloth for ironing. The support added by interfacing is great when you're stitching on thin fabrics, and it prevents over-tightened stitches from puckering the fabric. This material will seal thread tails if you add it after stitching. While you're stitching, interfacing can help keep the back of your work looking clean; simply angle your needle between the ground fabric and interfacing to bury tails.

Interfacing and fusible web

Fusible web is a paper-backed adhesive for fusing fabric, cardboard, or other porous materials, and it's often used in appliqué.

To back a piece of fabric with the adhesive, lay the rough, web-covered side of the paper on the wrong side of the fabric and iron according to manufacturer's directions. When the paper-backed fabric is cool, cut it to the desired shape, remove the paper backing and, with the web side face down on the item to be joined, iron to fuse the layers together. As with all craft products, test first and follow the manufacturer's directions for best results. Fusible web is also available on a spool and is sometimes not backed with paper; Stitch Witchery is a popular example, and is most often sold in a 1-inch (2.5-cm) wide roll.

■ TRANSFERRING PATTERNS

If you're working from colored patterns, transfer just the lines created by bordering colors and outlines. Refer to the patterns as you stitch for color placement. The more accurate your transfer is, the more time and frustration you will save while you work. Regardless of which transfer method you prefer, do not transfer a pattern while the fabric is stretched in an embroidery hoop because the design may be skewed when you remove the fabric.

There are an overwhelming number of ways to transfer patterns to fabric, and many products on the market are designed with embroidery projects in mind. I most frequently use iron-transfer pencils, fabric-marking pencils, interfacing, tissue paper, and one-step transfer pens. Remember that transferred lines will not be perfect and that you may need to fill in the gaps of a pattern by hand and retouch the lines while you stitch. As with all marking materials, first test on a scrap of fabric or in an inconspicuous area.

Air- and Water-Soluble Fabric-Marking Pens

These are the best tools for transferring designs to fabric because, as their name suggests, the ink is easily removed in water or will disappear over time with natural exposure to air. The fine-pointed tips of the pens help achieve crisp, detailed lines. Although air-soluble pens are time-sensitive (their marks disappear within hours or weeks depending on the pen), the lines are easy to retouch. A word of caution: some stitchers have found these marks showing up on fabric years after they thought the marks had disappeared.

Air-and-water-soluble fabric-marking pens are invaluable

Some pens are only air-soluble, only water-soluble, or both, and some pens are double-ended to combine these features. Do not use water-soluble pens on dry-clean-only fabrics. The ink from these pens is set by ironing and sometimes by direct sunlight; check manufacturer's directions and avoid ironing marked lines. Although marking pens are best for light and mid-color fabrics, high-quality white pens are available for dark fabrics and are generally a little more expensive than the most common blue and purple pens.

It is best to use a light source for transferring a pattern with these pens. Tape the pattern to either a window or light table and tape the fabric on top of the pattern; trace the lines of the pattern onto the fabric.

One-Step Transfer Pens

These pens are essentially water-soluble fabric-marking pens that let out a large stream of ink. To transfer a pattern with this pen, lay the pattern on the fabric and very slowly trace over the pattern. The design will be transferred as the ink bleeds through the pattern paper and onto the fabric. Drawing very slowly and using paper that's no thicker than typing paper will help ensure a successful transfer.

One-step transfer pen

Iron-Transfer Pens and Pencils

These utensils are usually wax-based, permanent (therefore best for the wrong side of the fabric), produce crisp lines when kept sharp, and do not require a light source. Simply draw over the pattern, lay the pattern face down on the fabric, and iron. Keep in mind that the reverse image will be transferred; if your design is not symmetrical, first hold the design to a light source and trace the lines to the back of the pattern. The amount of time you iron determines the thickness of the lines; test first to become familiar with the subtleties of each pen and pencil on scrap pieces of fabric before you make the final transfer. I prefer iron-transfer pencils over iron-transfer pens because the result tends to be more predictable.

Iron-transfer pens and pencils

Tailor's Chalk and Fabric-Marking Pencils

Tailor's chalk is best used for large, temporary marks and is easily removed with a small brush or water. The chalk is great for making quick marks on dark fabric and, as its name suggests, is most commonly used for garment sewing. The downside is that the marks are often too easily removed. Chalk is offered in many colors, with white and blue the most common, and in small bars (often called flakes), pencils, and in powdered form with the use of an applicator (often called Chaco liners). Some marking pencils are made of material similar to chalk; kept sharp, they may be used for thin lines and removed by washing or gently brushing fabric with a small, stiff-bristled paint brush. Marking pencils made of soapstone are great for marking dark fabrics; these hollow, refillable, clear marking pencils hold a round stick of soapstone that needs to be sharpened on sandpaper sheets that are sold with the pencils.

Tailor's chalk and fabric marking pencils

Graphite Pencils

Common wood and mechanical pencils are often overlooked as transfer tools. They are best used on light-colored fabric with light pressure. Do not expect to remove the marks; instead, stitch directly over the marks. If you are new to stitching and find it hard to stitch directly over a pattern, do not use a pencil as a transfer tool. Some frown on using pencils because thick pencil lines may dirty pale-colored threads. Faint lines may be removed with a mild soap and cold water.

Everyday pencils make good transfer tools

Dressmaker's Carbon

Some may find that dressmaker's carbon is difficult to work with because it's hard to achieve the thin lines required by detailed patterns. Although some brands are better than others, my experience is that the transferred lines almost always completely wear off before stitching is complete. However, many benefits still make dressmaker's carbon a viable tool for transferring patterns: Carbon paper is free of grease and wax, the marks made by most brands are not set by ironing, the pages are available in many colors and can be reused, and the markings are removed by laundering or with a fabric eraser. Sometimes, dressmaker's carbon is the most convenient way to transfer designs to thick, dark fabrics.

To transfer a pattern with dressmaker's carbon, tape the fabric to a hard, flat surface and tape the pattern on top. Carefully slide a piece of carbon paper face down between the layers and draw over the design with a stylus (or a knitting needle or ballpoint pen) or a tracing wheel (either smooth or serrated) that is often included in the package of tracing paper. Carefully remove the pattern paper and lift the carbon transfer paper.

Dressmaker's carbon is great for dark fabrics

Mesh Transfer Canvas

This material is a good replacement for dressmaker's carbon when you're using thick, heavy fabrics. The transfer method is similar to the traditional pricking and pouncing method in which holes are poked into pattern paper that is laid on top of fabric; a chalklike material is then rubbed over the surface of the pattern through the holes in the paper to the fabric below.

To use the mesh canvas, lay the clear, reusable sheet of thin plastic canvas on your design and trace the design onto the surface of the canvas with a washable marker or pen. Lay the canvas on top of the fabric on a hard surface and redraw over the pattern lines with an air- or water-soluble fabric-marking pen; allow the ink to seep through the holes of the canvas to the surface of the fabric. Remove the canvas and touch up the dotted pattern lines with the marking pen.

Fusible Interfacing

When a design is symmetrical (or is mirrored), it can be outlined from the back of the fabric by using lightweight interfacing. Tape the paper pattern to a hard, flat surface, center and tape the interfacing, fusible side down over the pattern, and trace the design lines with a permanent marker. Make sure to use a light-colored marker for light fabrics. Fuse the interfacing to the back of the fabric according to manufacturer's directions. Stitch with the pattern wrong side up in an embroidery hoop and keep the thread knots on the side of the fabric with the interfacing. Remember, many stitches are not reversible and should not be stitched from the wrong side of the fabric.

Tissue Paper
This method is great for working on dark, thick, and velvet fabrics. Simply lay tissue paper over the design and draw the pattern lines on top of the paper. With contrasting thread, baste the tissue paper onto the right side of the fabric along the design lines. Once all design lines have been stitched, lightly wet the tissue paper and tear the paper off. Embroider on top of the transferred lines; if the basting stitches show when you've completed the embroidery, remove the basting stitches from the back of the fabric.

■ EMBROIDERY HOOPS AND FRAMES
Embroidery hoops are very affordable and essential to most projects. They are designed to keep fabric taut between two rings of wood, plastic, or metal while you stitch. The most common classic-style hoop, typically made of wood or plastic, uses a screw to tighten the outer ring. Hoops that have an inner metal ring that fits inside a plastic outer ring are used for both hand and machine embroidery, like the classic-style hoop, but are best used for machine embroidery.

You'll need different sized hoops for different sized projects

To mount fabric in a classic-style hoop for hand embroidery, lay the inner ring on a flat surface, center the design to be stitched over the ring, and lay the outer ring of the hoop directly over the inner ring to sandwich the fabric; press down with even pressure and tighten the screw. When you're retightening the hoop during stitching, be sure to pull the fabric evenly from all sides, keeping the warp and weft threads at a 90-degree angle. To prepare fabric for machine embroidery in this classic-style hoop, mount the fabric with the inner ring on top of the fabric. Doing so allows the fabric to be in direct contact with both the presser foot and needle plate (see page 109 for sewing machine diagram).

To secure fabric in the metal and plastic hoop for hand embroidery, lay the plastic outer ring on a flat surface, lay the fabric face down over the hoop with the design centered, and mount the metal ring inside the plastic ring (thus sandwiching the fabric) by squeezing together the two metal arms that extend from the ring. Turn the hoop over to begin stitching. To mount fabric in the same style hoop for machine embroidery, lay the plastic outer ring on a flat surface, center the design to be stitched face up over the ring, and set the metal ring. The metal arms help you hold onto the hoop while you're doing machine embroidery but it sometimes catches your threads when it's used for hand embroidery.

It is best to use a hoop that is larger in diameter than the motif to be stitched so that the fabric does not need to be moved during stitching and stitches are not pressed between the rings. However, following this rule is not always possible when you're working large projects. To protect stitches, wrap the inner wood or plastic ring of your embroidery hoop (Figure 1) with a 1-inch (2.5-cm) strip of fabric (do not wrap the inner ring if it is metal). When the ring is completely covered, overlap the first few wraps and whipstitch (see page 103) the end of the strip to the fabric on the inside of the ring. The fabric-wrapped inner ring will also keep your fabric taut in the hoop and allow you to pin ribbons and other strips of fabric to the fabric while you stitch; this feature is extremely important when you're stitching the velvet ribbons on page 48 because the outer ring of the hoop may crush the velvet.

Figure 1

Embroidery frames, offered in laptop and tabletop styles, are best used for needlepoint, other counted-thread techniques, and any time it is crucial to keep fabric evenly stretched. All the projects in this book may be stitched without the use of a frame.

■ THIMBLES AND NEEDLE PULLERS

Thimbles protect fingers

Thimbles protect your fingertips from accidental contact with the needle and help you to push the needle through the fabric. Thimbles are most commonly made of metal and designed to be worn on the tip of the middle finger of the stitching hand. The dimples in the surface hold the needle in place while your finger pushes the needle through the fabric. The key to working with a thimble is finding one that fits snugly enough to stay on your finger but still feels comfortable. Thimbles are sold in various sizes, including mini/petite, small, small/medium, medium, medium/large, and large. To make a customized thimble, see page 22. Other thimbles include tailor's thimbles with extra deep dimples, thimble rings that do not require a perfect fit because they slide over the first knuckle, leather thimbles with small metal disks that pad the finger, and small metal disks that adhere directly to your skin. If you are new to embroidery and find it difficult to manage a thimble, consider not using one—I have never used a thimble and have not experienced any problems with sore fingertips.

Needle pullers are a great help for tired hands. No matter how well you choose your needle size, you will sometimes run into an area where it is difficult to pull the needle through dense stitches or back your needle out of a tough spot. Labeled as Quilter's Needle Pullers, these small, round rubber disks help tired hands grip needles. There are also small plastic tubes, called Needle Tuggers, which fit over the needle and grip the needle when they're squeezed.

Needle pullers help tired hands

■ NEEDLES

As you become familiar with embroidery you will not need to worry about choosing the perfect needle size; the choice will come to you naturally for the project at hand. However, it is very important to choose the correct needles and know the basics of needle sizing. Needles differ in size, sharpness, and in the length of the eye (the hole for the thread). Generally, the larger the number, the thinner and shorter the needle—but there are a few exceptions: size 15 and 18 sharps are larger than sizes 1 through 10, and darners, sizes 14 through 18, are larger than sizes 1 through 19. Sharps (general sewing needles), quilting (also called betweens), leather, and ballpoint sewing needles all have small, round eyes, whereas darners and needles for embroidery (or crewel), tapestry, chenille, and beading all have long eyes. For tips on choosing beading needles, see page 56. It is best to test your needle size with the number of strands and fabric before you start a project.

Different projects require different needles

Get to know the size of your needles

If you are just getting started and do not want to invest in an entire set of needles, most beginning embroidery projects can be made with a pack of embroidery needles (including sizes 1 to 10), a few tapestry needles (even sizes 16 to 28) and a couple of chenille needles (sizes 20 and 26). You will be able to choose the correct needle for almost any project (and all the projects in this book) if you understand the basic sizing of embroidery and tapestry needles.

In discussing needle sizes, I've assumed that you are working on one layer of medium-weight fabric like muslin, linen, or quilter's cotton. You may need to change needles to work with thicker or thinner fabric. If you have trouble pulling the threaded eye of a needle through thick or multiple layers of fabric, try using a needle that is one size larger. If you notice that your needle is leaving holes in the fabric, your needle is too large; try a smaller one.

Store needles in a needle book with wool felt pages, in a pincushion, needle case, or strawberry emery. The material in cloth strawberries (found at craft stores and often sold with tomato pincushions) sharpens needles. Wool felt pages (like the ones in this book you can make on page 16), lightly coat stored needles with lanolin, which prevents corrosion.

If you have trouble threading needles, use a needle threader. Insert the metal loop in the eye of the needle, thread the wire loop, and pull the needle threader back through the eye of the needle. Trimming thread at an angle with a sharp pair of scissors before threading the needle also helps you find the eye of the needle. If you become frustrated threading a needle, try using a larger needle with a longer eye or try threading the needle from the opposite side of the eye (one side of the needle's eye may be easier to thread due to the factory processes of forming and punching). See page 46 for tips on threading a needle with wool thread.

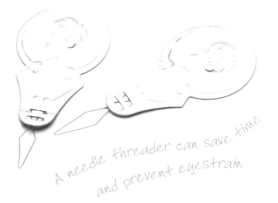

A needle threader can save time and prevent eyestrain

For a general guide to choosing needles for the sewing machine, see page 109.

Embroidery

These needles, also called crewel needles, are the same length as sharps (general sewing needles) but their larger eyes accommodate multiple strands of thread. The sharp points are suitable for piercing tightly woven fabric. The sizes range from 1 to 12, with 12 being the smallest. When you're working with stranded (typically sold as six strands) cotton thread—also called floss—use a size 10 needle for one strand, a size 8 needle for three strands, and a size 3 needle for six strands. When you're working with pearl cotton (such as DMC Numbers 5 and 8), use a size 6 needle for No. 5 thread and a size 8 needle for No. 8 thread. If you find that you prefer shorter needles, try working with quilting (betweens) needles, but keep in mind that the small round eyes may be difficult to thread.

Tapestry

These needles have a blunt end designed to slip between the threads of the fabric as opposed to piercing the surface and are thus most often used for needlepoint worked on canvas and other counted-thread work. When you're working stitches into a foundation row of threads, as with detached buttonhole stitch (page 102), the blunt end prevents you from splitting the threads of the ground stitches. The needles' large eyes accommodate tapestry wool, pearl cotton, and six-strand threads. The sizes range from 13 to 28, with 28 being the finest. As a general rule, use a size 16 or 18 needle for working with tapestry wool. When you're working stranded cotton thread, use a size 26 needle for one or two strands, a size 24 needle for three or four strands, and a size 22 needle for six strands. When you're working with pearl cotton, use a size 22 needle for No. 5 thread and a size 26 needle for No. 8 thread. If you like the size of tapestry needles, but prefer to work with a sharper needle, try working with chenille needles. You often need the large size and sharpness of chenille needles to work with very thick fabrics or silk ribbons.

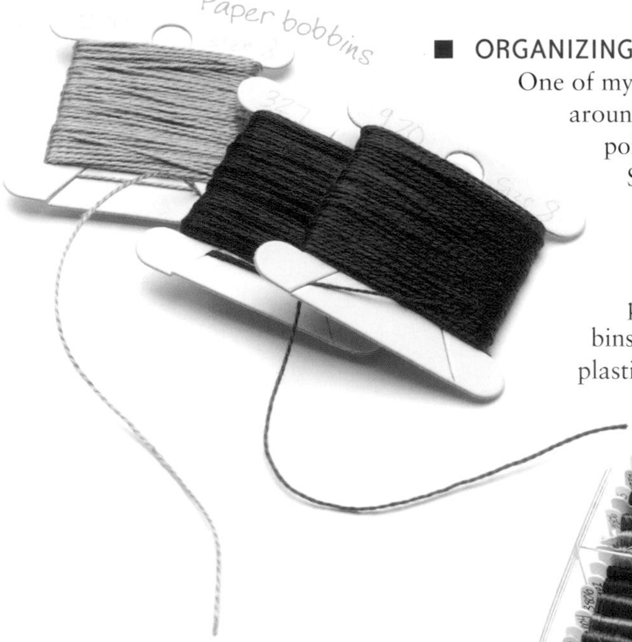

Paper bobbins

■ ORGANIZING, MANAGING, AND BLENDING THREADS

One of my favorite ways to store and organize threads is by wrapping them around flat paper bobbins (also available in plastic), then using a fine-point permanent marker to label the bobbins with their color number. Some stitchers prefer not to use this method because tightly wound bobbins may leave creases in the thread. The clear plastic cases made to hold these types of bobbins make threads extremely easy to find. The small winders often sold in packages with bobbins simplify the task of filling the bobbins. Stitch-Bows are long, plastic bobbins that do not require the thread to be rewound and are available with plastic pages for storage in a three-ring binder.

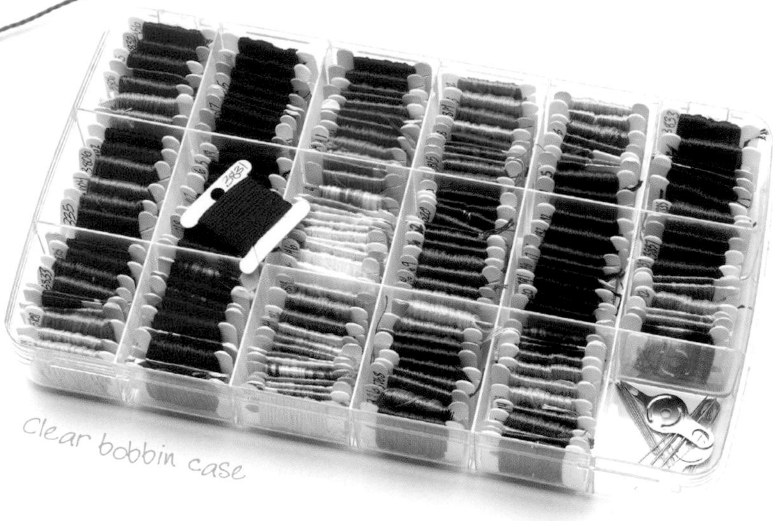

Clear bobbin case

Your threads will be more manageable if you keep them less than 20 inches (50.8 cm) long. Long threads tangle easily, require more arm motion, and are difficult to blend with other colors. For those who like to work with even shorter strands, remove the two paper wrappers on a new skein of six-strand cotton thread and cut one end loop to create ready-to-use, uniformly sized, 12-inch (30.5-cm) lengths of thread. If you are working with threads that tangle easily or tend to snag, use a thread

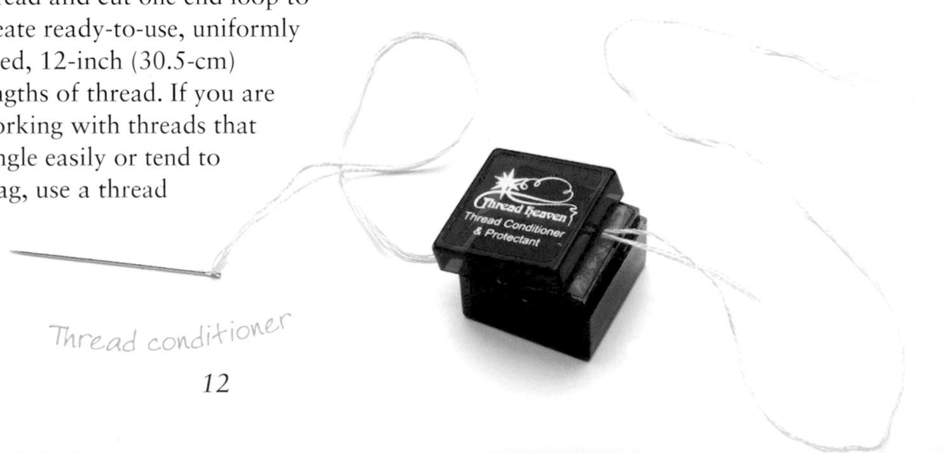

Thread conditioner

12

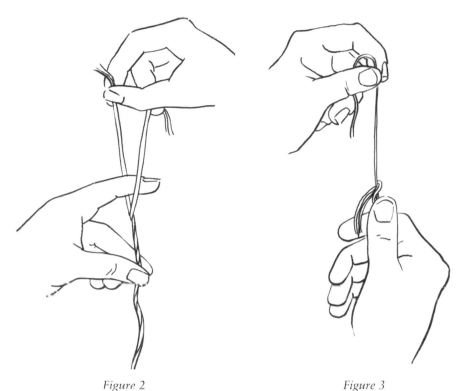

Figure 2   Figure 3

conditioner to lightly coat the strands; simply hold the thread against the conditioner, or between the grooves in the conditioner's case, and lightly drag the thread through. A conditioner like Thread Heaven, which is acid-free and nontoxic, keeps threads feeling light, whereas beeswax and other wax-based conditioners sometimes leave a thick film on threads.

To blend strands, you must first know the two general methods for separating them. The first way is to hold a 12- to 20-inch (30.5- to 50.8-cm) piece of stranded thread in one hand, with the strand(s) you want between your thumb and index finger, and the remaining strands held against the palm of your hand with your other fingers; separate the strands with your other hand according to Figure 2; allow the strands to slowly untwist.

The second way (and the method I prefer) is called stripping (Figure 3): Start with a 12- to 20-inch (30.5- to 50.8-cm) piece of stranded thread, grab one strand and pull it directly up and out of the bundle, straightening the remaining bundles of threads with your other hand as you pull. Repeat until you have removed the desired number of threads.

Now that you have the strands separated, join them with other extracted strands of different colors to create a "blended needle."

■ START STITCHING: BEGINNING AND ENDING THREADS

Begin by threading the needle with a needle threader or wet the thread before you slide it through the eye of the needle. Double-knot one thread tail; do not knot the ends together. Bring the needle up from the wrong side of the fabric. Many stitchers prefer not to use knots to start a new thread because knots sometimes clutter the back and make it difficult to pull the needle to the wrong side. Instead, they hold onto a 2-inch (5.1-cm) tail and stitch over the tail as they work the design, or they weave the thread into the back of previous stitches. See the waste-knot technique on page 27 if you wish to avoid using knots.

When a design is complete or your thread runs out, take the needle to the wrong side of the fabric, make a small stitch next to the base of the thread, and pull the needle to create a loop; insert the needle through the loop and pull taut to knot. Repeat. If you do not secure the tail of a thread with a knot, weave the needle through the back of several previous stitches; pull the thread taut and trim.

For more tips on how to begin and end threads and manage thread tails, including the waste-knot technique, see Hiding Knots and Thread Tails on page 27. If you need to fix a mistake, use a seam ripper or embroidery scissors to trim the incorrect stitches on the wrong side of the fabric. If you need help removing trimmed threads, try a pair of tweezers.

Seam rippers are great for removing mistakes

THE TOOLS NO EMBROIDERER SHOULD BE WITHOUT

Bobbins for storing and labeling threads
Dressmaker's carbon and tracing wheel
Embroidery hoops
Embroidery scissors
Fabric-marking pens and pencils
Needles
Needle book or needle case
Needle pulling disks
Pins and safety pins
Rotary cutter, self-healing cutting mat, and a large clear ruler
Seam ripper and tweezers
Tape measure and ruler
Thread conditioner
Thimble(s)

THREAD CONVERSION CHART

Color	DMC #/Name	Anchor #	Color	DMC #/Name	Anchor #
	Blanc	1		919 Red Copper	340
	Ecru	387		920 Medium Copper	884
	150 Ultra Very Dark Dusty Rose	59		921 Copper	5975
	221 Very Dark Shell Pink	897		922 Light Copper	1003
	310 Black	403		924 Very Dark Gray Green	851
	327 Dark Violet	100		3011 Dark Khaki Green	846
	471 Very Light Avocado Green	266		3013 Light Khaki Green	842
	472 Ultra Light Avocado Green	253		3051 Dark Green Gray	681
	501 Dark Blue Green	878		3052 Medium Green Gray	262
	597 Turquoise	1064		3346 Hunter Green	267
	613 Very Light Drab Brown	956		3347 Medium Yellow Green	266
	676 Light Old Gold	891		3364 Pine Green	260
	704 Bright Chartreuse	256		3371 Black Brown	382
	712 Cream	926		3685 Very Dark Mauve	1028
	738 Very Light Tan	361		3740 Dark Antique Violet	873
	739 Ultra Very Light Tan	387		3768 Dark Gray Green	779
	742 Light Tangerine	303		3803 Dark Mauve	69
	743 Medium Yellow	302		3811 Very Light Turquoise	1060
	745 Light Pale Yellow	300		3819 Light Moss Green	278
	807 Peacock Blue	168		3830 Terra Cotta	5975
	814 Dark Garnet	45		3854 Medium Autumn Gold	313
	815 Medium Garnet	43		3855 Light Autumn Gold	311
	838 Very Dark Beige Brown	1088			

STITCH REFERENCE
AND NEEDLE STORAGE

BOOK

Learn and practice stitches on these pages made of wool felt, then combine them into a clever little book. Add a table of contents, needles, and needle threaders and you'll have a book for your needles that also serves as a reference book of your stitches. Two further bonuses: the lanolin in the wool of the felt pages keeps your needles from corroding and the book comes in handy while you're working on other projects.

■ SIZE

3½ × 3 inches (8.9 × 7.6 cm)

■ THREADS

100% cotton 6-strand embroidery threads (I used DMC Embroidery Floss Article 117), 8.7 yards (8 m)/skein, 1 skein each of #472 ultra light avocado green, #676 light old gold, #919 red copper, #921 copper, #3685 very dark mauve, and #3768 dark gray green

■ FABRIC

100% wool felt: dark sage green, 4 × 3½ inches (10.2 × 8.9 cm), 6 pieces; 100% cotton: 2 coordinating prints, 4 × 3½ inches (10.2 × 8.9 cm), 3 pieces of 1 print and 4 pieces of the other; 100% cotton: 4 × 3½ inches (10.2 × 8.9 cm), 2 coordinating light colors, 1 piece of each; 100% cotton: coordinating light color (I used yellow), 11 × 8½ inches (27.9 × 21.6 cm), 1 piece

■ NOTIONS

Medium-weight nonwoven fusible web, 4 × 3½ inches (10.2 × 8.9 cm), with a 1½-inch (3.8-cm) square opening placed ⅛ inch (3 mm) right of center, 6 pieces, and 1 piece without a square cut out of the center; heavyweight nonwoven fusible web, 11 × 8½ inches (27.9 × 21.6 cm), 1 piece; needles, in an assortment of sizes (I used tapestry sizes 20 and 24, embroidery sizes 3, 6, 8, and 10, chenille size 20, quilting size 10, and beading size 10); clear ruler; awl or pushpin; self-healing cutting mat or 4-inch (10.2-cm) square piece of cardboard; ribbon, 100% silk, ⅛ inch (3mm) wide, olive green, 5 inches (12.7 cm) long, 6 pieces; fabric-marking pen or pencil

■ STITCHES

Backstitch, page 20
Bookbinding stitch, page 19
Chain stitch, page 21
Couching, page 21
Double running stitch, page 20
French knots, page 21
Long-and-short satin stitch, page 20
Overcast stitch, page 21
Satin stitch, page 20
Seed stitch, 20
Split stitch, 21
Stem stitch, 21
Straight and running stitch, page 20

A safe place to stash needles

• Stitches •
Running stitch
Double running stitch
Seed stitch
Backstitch
Satin stitch
Long-and-short satin stitch
Stem stitch
Split stitch
Overcast stitch
Couching
Chain stitch
French Knots

To construct the book's six pages, fuse the six 4- × 3½-inch (10.2- × 8.9-cm) pieces of fusible web (with the squares cut out of the center) to the wrong side of six of the patterned and solid-colored 4- × 3½-inch (10.2- × 8.9-cm) pieces of fabric according to manufacturer's directions. Set aside the three remaining 4- × 3½-inch (10.2- × 8.9-cm) pieces of fabric; one piece is for the cover and two pieces are for the back page. Peel off the paper backing and fuse the 4- × 3½-inch (10.2- × 8.9-cm) pieces of fabric to the six pieces of felt by ironing the two fabrics with wrong side facing. Alternate between colors and patterns. For the back page, use the remaining 4- × 3½-inch (10.2- × 8.9-cm) piece of fusible web (without the hole cut in the center) to fuse two of the 4-× 3½-inch (10.2-× 8.9-cm) remaining fabric pieces together with wrong sides facing. Trim ¼ inch (6 mm) off all sides of the pieces to even the edges. Orient the felt pages so that the square cut in the fusible web is slightly right of center (the binding will cover the extra space on the left side).

To fill the book, practice one stitch at the top and one stitch at the bottom of each page using two to four strands of thread; leave room in the center of the page for needle and pin storage and ¼ inch (6 mm) along the left side for binding. Experiment with thread color blends, number of strands, and needle size (see page

10 for a guide to choosing needles) to become familiar with your needles and design effects. To create loops for the needle threaders, place the needle threaders on one of the felt pages and make two horizontal, ¼-inch (6-mm) long stitches over the base of the needle threaders (to make my stitches, I braided six strands of 100 percent cotton for durability). The back of each page remains exposed to help you identify, select, and understand how stitches are made; keep the thread tails trimmed.

To make the inside front cover's title page, fuse the 11- × 8½-inch (27.9- × 21.6-cm) piece of heavyweight fusible web to the same-size piece of fabric; trim the edges if necessary. Type the list of stitches in the order they were stitched and size the font, line spacing, and point size to fit in a 3- × 2¼-inch (7.6- × 5.7-cm) rectangle. Print the list on the fabric by feeding the paper-backed fabric through an ink-jet or bubble-jet printer. This process may be difficult for some printers; see page 67 for alternate iron-transfer and fabric-printing instructions. If you choose not to type the list, simply write the stitch names with a fine-point permanent marker. Trim the piece of fabric to 4 × 3½ inches (10.2 × 8.9 cm); leave an extra ½ inch (1.3 cm) along the right side of the page to accommodate the binding. Fuse the title page to the remaining 4- × 3½-inch (10.2- × 8.9-cm) piece of fabric to make the front cover and trim ¼ inch (6 mm) off all edges of the fabric. The text of the title page should be around ¼ inch (6 mm) from the edge of the fabric on the top, bottom, and left side.

Lay one stitched page with the felt side down on the cutting mat or cardboard and lay the ruler on top of and parallel with the left side and ¼ inch (6 mm) from the left edge. Using the marking pen or pencil and starting at the top of the page, mark six dots down the length of the page that are ½ inch (1.3 cm) apart and ¼ inch (6 mm) from the left edge. Remove the ruler and, with the awl or push-pin, punch small holes in place of the dots. Mark and punch holes in the five remaining fused felt pages, front cover, and back page. Stack the pages and bind with the largest tapestry needle by pulling a 5-inch (12.7-cm) piece of ribbon (or five to six strands of various thread colors) through one set of holes, pulling tight, knotting twice, and trimming the tails; repeat five more times. For a cleaner look and sturdier binding, refer to the bookbinding stitch below.

HOW TO BIND A BOOK

Use this simple bookbinding stitch to securely and pro-fessionally finish your needle book. This stitch is basic to bookmakers and those who make journals.

To begin, thread a size 20 tapestry needle with six to eight strands of embroidery floss. Come up from the back at 1 and leave a 3-inch (7.6-cm) tail. Loop over the top of the book and come up at 2. Go around the spine and come up at 2 again. Insert the needle at 3, go around the spine, and insert at 3 again. Come up at 4, go around the spine, and come up at 4 again. Insert the needle at 5, go around the spine, and insert at 5 again. Come up at 6, go around the spine, and come up at 6 again. Insert the needle at 7, go around the spine, and insert at 7 again. Bring up around the end and insert at 7. Work back to the top with running stitches: Bring the needle up at 6, insert at 5, bring up at 4, insert at 3, bring up at 2, insert at 1, go around the spine and insert at 1 again. Knot the working thread with the starting tail twice and hide the threads in the pages of the book.

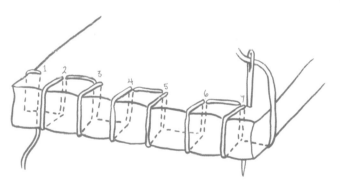

The bookbinding stitch holds together any book

STITCHES

Straight stitch and running stitch

Working from right to left, make a straight stitch by bringing the needle up and insert at 1, ⅛ to ¼ inch (3 to 6 mm) from the starting point. To make a line of running stitches (a row of straight stitches worked one after the other), bring the needle up at 2 and repeat.

Double running stitch

This stitch is simply two passes of running stitches with the second pass of running stitches filling in the spaces left by the first pass. Insert the needle into the holes created by the first pass of stitches.

Seed stitch

This stitch may be worked in any direction with small, randomly placed straight stitches. Bring the needle up at 1 and insert at 2. For bolder seed stitches, take two stitches parallel and close to each other to place the "seeds" in pairs.

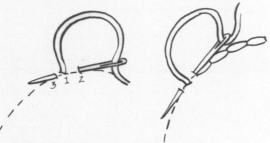

Backstitch

Working from right to left, bring the needle up at 1 and insert behind the starting point at 2. Bring the needle up at 3, repeat by inserting at 1, and bring the needle up at a point that is a stitch length beyond 3.

Satin stitch

Generally worked from left to right, this stitch is used to fill shapes. Bring the needle up at 1, insert at 2, and bring back up at 3. Repeat. For variations on this stitch, see page 31.

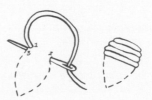

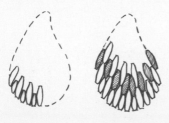

Long-and-short satin stitch

Like satin stitch, this stitch is used to fill shapes. Work the first row of stitches from left to right along the outside edge of a shape and stitch a row with long and short vertical stitches; alternate between ⅛- and ¼-inch (3- and 6-mm) long stitches. To work the next rows, add ¼-inch (6-mm) long stitches above the foundation row, filling in the spaces left by the previous row according to the illustration. Create shading by switching colors every row or every few rows. The exact stitch size is determined by the size of the motif to be filled and the thread(s) used.

Stem stitch

Working from left to right, bring the needle up at 1 and insert the needle ⅛ to ¼ inch (3 to 6 mm) away at 2. Bring the needle up half-way between 1 and 2, at 3. Keep the newly created loop below the needle and stitched line before pulling it taut. Repeat by inserting the needle ⅛ to ¼ inch (3 to 6 mm) to the right and bring up at 2.

Split stitch

Working from left to right in the same manner as stem stitch (see above), bring the needle up at 1, insert at 2, and bring up near the right end of the previous stitch (between 1 and 2, at 3), inserting the needle into the thread to split the thread in two. When you're working with multiple strands of thread, insert the needle between the strands.

Overcast stitch

Working from right to left, tightly work satin stitches over one or more couched (laid) threads or row of stitches. Bring the working thread up at 1, insert at 2, and bring up at 3. This stitch may also be worked from left to right and with a base of running, back-, split, chain, or stem stitches.

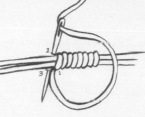

Couching

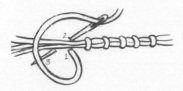

Working from right to left, use one thread, known as the couching or working thread, to tack down one or more laid threads, known as the couched threads. Bring the working thread up at 1 and insert at 2, over the laid threads to tack them down; repeat by inserting the needle at 3. This stitch may also be worked from left to right, and the spacing between the couching threads may vary for different design effects.

Chain stitch

Working from top to bottom, bring the needle up at 1 and reinsert at 1 to create a loop; do not pull the thread taut. Bring the needle up at 2, through the loop, and gently pull the needle toward you to pull the loop flush to the fabric. Repeat by reinserting at 2 to create another loop and bring the needle up at 3. To finish a row of stitches, tack down the last loop with a short straight stitch.

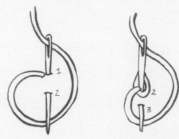

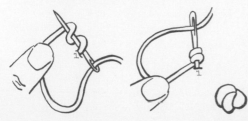

French knots

Bring the needle up at 1 and hold the thread taut about 2 inches (5.1 cm) above the fabric, point the needle toward your fingers, and move the needle in a circular motion to wrap the thread around the needle one or two times. Insert the needle into the fabric near 1 and complete by holding the thread taut near the knot, according to the illustration, as you pull the needle and thread through the knot and fabric.

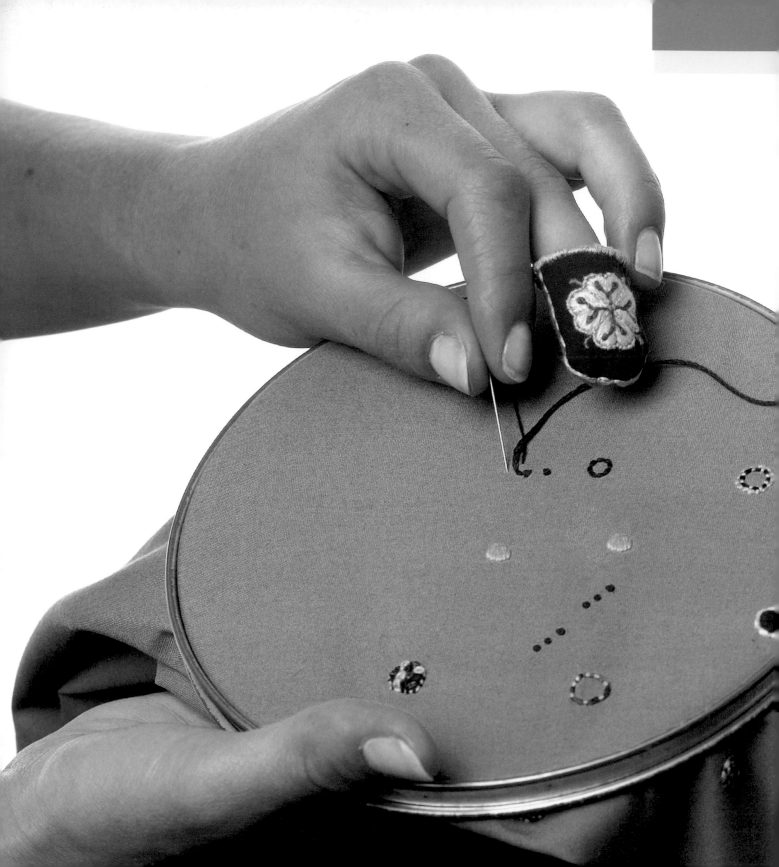

SPECIFICATIONS

■ SIZE

1⅛ ×
1 inch (2.9
× 2.5 cm)
Specifi-
cations
shown for
all four
thimbles
(adjust
quantities
as neces-
sary)

■ THREADS

100% cot-
ton 6-strand
embroidery
threads (I used
DMC Embroi-
dery Floss,
Article 117),
8.7 yards
(8 m)/skein, 1
skein each of
the colors list-
ed in the keys;
sewing thread,
orange

■ FABRIC

For facing: 100% cotton,
purple, yellow, red,
and green, 8 × 8 inches
(20.3 × 20.3 cm),
1 piece each color;
For backing: 100%
cotton, orange and
purple, 4 × 4 inches
(10.2 × 10.2 cm), 1 piece
of each color; red,
4 × 4 inches (10.2 ×
10.2 cm), 2 pieces;
Leather: ¹/₁₆ inch (1.5 mm)
thick, light brown, cut to
inner solid line of the
pattern, 4 pieces

■ NOTIONS

Medium-weight
nonwoven fusible
web, 2 × 2 inches
(5.1 × 5.1 cm),
8 pieces; needles,
embroidery sizes
3 and 10; embroi-
dery hoop,
6 inches (15.2 cm)
in diameter; fabric-
marking pen or
pencil; liquid seam
sealant (like Fray
Check)
Optional: sewing
machine

■ STITCHES

Couching, page 21
Double running stitch,
page 20
French knots, page 21
Long-and-short satin
stitch, page 20
Overcast stitch, page 21
Running stitch, page 20
Satin stitch, page 20
Satin stitch over double
running stitch, page 30
Straight stitch, page 20
Whipped stem stitch,
page 24
Optional: Bound satin
stitch, page 81

KOREAN-INSPIRED
THIMBLES

Fun, decorative, and functional, embroidered thimbles make welcome additions to
every sewing basket. Lined with leather on
one side, these Korean-inspired thimbles are
durable and comfortable. After you make
one, you'll want to make the entire set—and
then more for friends and relatives.

■ INSTRUCTIONS

Note: The pattern is for a size small/medium thimble; for more information on thimbles, see page 9. If you find that the first thimble you make is too small or large, adjust the size of the pattern in ⅛-inch (3-mm) increments. For slight adjustments, move toward the inside or outside edge the machine-stitched (or double-running-stitched) seam (represented by the dashed line on the pattern) that joins the front and back pieces.

Using one of the transfer methods on pages 5–8, transfer one motif to the center of each 8-inch (20.3-cm) fabric square, matching the motif with the fabric color indicated with the patterns. Unless otherwise noted, work all stitches with one strand of thread and the size 10 embroidery needle. Use the size 3 needle to work with the six-strand couched threads. Refer to the patterns for color placement.

Purple thimble pattern

#150 ultra very dark dusty rose

#922 light copper

#3346 hunter green

#3811 very light turquoise

#3854 medium autumn gold

■ PURPLE THIMBLE

Mount the 8-inch (20.3-cm) square of purple fabric in the hoop. Use double running stitch and #3346 to outline the flower stem and work satin stitches horizontally across the stem to cover the double running stitches. Satin-stitch from the center of the leaves out toward the edges at a 45-degree angle with #3854. Add highlights on top of the previous stitches with #922 and straight stitch. Make horizontal satin stitches for the bottom two pink stripes of the flower and vertical satin stitches for the top pink stripe with #150. Top off the flower with four French knots in #3811. Fill in the spaces between the pink stripes by couching down one strand of #3811 with one strand of the same color thread. Remove the fabric from the hoop.

Green thimble pattern

#327 dark violet

#472 ultra light avocado green

#814 dark garnet

■ GREEN THIMBLE

Mount the 8-inch (20.3-cm) square of green fabric in the hoop. Use double running stitch and #472 to outline the petals. Starting from the bottom point of the petals, fan satin stitches toward the outside edges, covering the double running stitches. To outline the petals, bring #814 up at the bottom point of one

WHIPPED STEM STITCH

Work a line with stem stitches (see page 21). Bring the needle up at the start of the line and wrap the stitches by slipping the needle under the stem stitches from the top so you don't pierce the fabric. Wrap each stem stitch only once for a uniform, balanced look.

petal, couch down with the same colored thread along the edge of the satin stitches, and bring the thread back through the fabric at the base of the petal; repeat for all petals. Add highlights on top of the base of the petals with two to three short, straight stitches and #327. Stitch the accent lines between the petals with stem stitch and #814; add highlights with #327 to create a whipped stem stitch. Remove the fabric from the hoop.

■ RED THIMBLE

Mount the 8-inch (20.3-cm) square of red fabric in the hoop. Use double running stitch and #472 to outline the petals. Cover the double running stitches and fill in the petals with satin stitches that extend from the base of the purple Y out toward the outside edges at a 45-degree angle. With #327, stitch the Y with three short, straight stitches on top of the petals and stitch one French knot at the top points of the Y. With one strand of #597, couch down two strands of thread with the same color around each flower petal as indicated on the pattern. With #922, make one French knot in the center of the flower and use overcast stitch for the remaining accent lines that surround the petals. Remove the fabric from the hoop.

■ YELLOW THIMBLE

Mount the 8-inch (20.3-cm) square of yellow fabric in the hoop. First use double running stitch to outline the petals, stem, and leaf with the colors indicated on the pattern; use the same color thread to cover the outlines with satin stitch. Accent the stem with #501 by taking three small horizontal stitches on the lower half of the stem. Accent the five central petals with #676 and #501, using one straight stitch of each color. Stitch one French knot in the center of the flower using #676. Remove the fabric from the hoop.

■ ASSEMBLING THE THIMBLES

Make a pattern by photocopying the thimble template (right) and trim along the outer line. To prepare the embroidered side, center the pattern over one of the stitched motifs and trace around the edge of the paper pattern with the marking pen or pencil. With the embroidery right-side down on a terry-cloth towel, fold the fabric with wrong sides facing along the bottom straight line and press. Insert one of the 2-inch (5.1-cm) squares of fusible web into the fold of the fabric face down until it meets the crease and is centered over the stitched motif. Follow manufacturer's directions to iron the fabric with the fusible web sandwiched between the layers. Unfold the fabric and peel off the paper of the fusible web; refold and fuse the two layers together with the embroidery right side down on the towel. Trim along the solid line of the pattern. Use two strands of any contrasting color of thread in the size 3 needle to baste a line (using temporary running stitches) that is 1/8 inch (3 mm) from the outer edge and indicated by the dashed line on the pattern.

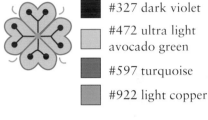

Red thimble pattern

■	#327 dark violet
■	#472 ultra light avocado green
■	#597 turquoise
■	#922 light copper

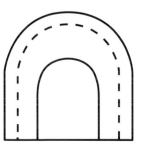

Yellow thimble pattern

■	#471 very light avocado green
■	#501 dark blue green
■	#676 light old gold
■	#815 medium garnet
■	#902 very dark garnet
■	#3740 dark antique violet
■	#3803 dark mauve
■	#3830 terra cotta

Thimble template

25

To prepare the backing, fold one of the contrasting 4-inch (10.2-cm) squares of fabric (use red for the purple thimble, purple for the green thimble, orange for the red thimble, and red for the yellow thimble) in half with wrong sides facing; press. Insert one of the 2-inch (5.1-cm) squares of fusible web into the fold of the fabric face down until it meets the crease and is centered. Follow manufacturer's directions to iron the fabric with the fusible web sandwiched between the layers. Unfold the fabric and peel off the paper of the fusible web; refold. Insert and center one piece of leather in the fold with the straight end aligned with the fold until it meets the crease; fuse the two layers together to secure the piece of leather. Center the pattern over the fabric with the bottom edge of the pattern flush with the fold of the fabric and draw around the outside edge of the pattern; trim along the outside line and use any contrasting color of thread to baste a line that is $\frac{1}{8}$ inch (3 mm) in from the outer edge (indicated by the dashed line on the pattern).

Stack the front and back pieces with right sides facing and baste together, using the first basted line as a guide and two strands of contrasting thread in the size 3 needle. With the sewing thread, machine stitch (or hand stitch with tightly spaced double running or backstitches) along the basted lines to secure the seam. Remove all basting threads and lightly cover the raw edges with liquid seam sealant. Turn the thimble right-side out by pinching the tip and rolling down the bottom edge; use a knitting needle or chopstick to smooth out the seam allowance inside the thimble. Repeat assembly instructions for the remaining pieces of fabric.

Finish the thimbles by couching down six strands of thread over the seams with one strand of thread. For the purple thimble, couch down a blend of four strands of #3854 and two strands of #922 with one strand of #3854; for the green thimble, couch down a blend of one strand of #814 and five strands of #472 with one strand of #472; for the red thimble, couch down six strands of #3766 with one strand of the same color thread; for the yellow thimble, couch down six strands of #3740 with one strand of the same color thread. If desired, embellish the bottom edge of the thimbles. (I finished the red thimble with bound satin stitch [page 81] and two strands of #597; for the yellow thimble, I continued the couching threads that covered the seam around the bottom edge.) Be sure to hide all knots on the inside of the thimbles, tucked inside the seam allowances.

A fun assortment of cheery thimbles

HIDING KNOTS AND THREAD TAILS

When you're starting and stopping stitching, it is important to hide thread tails for both neatness and security. Loose tails that are accidentally pulled may distort a design and weaken the stitches. Here are a few tips on how to manage thread tails:

• With the waste-knot technique it is almost impossible to find the starting point of the thread, and the technique helps create smooth, tidy, reversible stitches. Tie a knot in the end of the thread and insert the needle into the right side of the fabric in the center of an area or line that will later be covered with stitches, about ¼ inch (6 mm) from the point where the first stitch will be taken. Take two to three small backstitches at the base of the knot and begin stitching. Trim off the knot and cover the backstitches as you complete the motif. You may end your stitching with a small knot on the back of the fabric (as directed below) or pull the thread through the back of previous stitches before you trim the thread tail.

• Similar to the waste-knot technique in that the starting tails of the thread are concealed and help make your fabric reversible, this technique is faster because the knot does not have to be trimmed off: Bring the thread up in the center of the motif or line from the back and stitch over the knot as you fill the motif. When you're starting a new thread or finishing a thread, hide tails and knots by inserting the needle at an angle under the previous stitches; satin stitches are great at concealing knots.

• When you're starting stitching on the fabric's edge or hem, knot the thread and take the first stitch about ¼ inch (6 mm) away from the starting point of the motif; make small running stitches in the seam allowance (or other concealed part of the fabric) until you reach the motif. You may also hide the knot and thread tail by inserting the needle between the layers of fabric of a hem; pull the thread taut with a quick yank to pull the knot close to the outer layer of fabric.

• Keep your knots small when you are finished stitching on the edge of an item by taking a few running stitches on the back of the fabric to an unexposed area. For a small yet strong knot, take a small stitch near the point where the needle came out of the fabric and pull to create a loop; insert the needle in the loop and pull taut. Repeat and trim the thread tail.

• Once you have built a foundation of stitches, you do not need to use a knot when you start a new thread. Instead, start by weaving the needle between previous stitches on the wrong side of the fabric, pull the thread through so that there is only a 2-inch (5.1-cm) tail, and hold the tail while you take the first couple of stitches.

CUDDLE-UP CORDUROY
COAT

Express your inner artist by dressing up the back of a new coat or updating an old favorite with a vibrant motif inspired by folk art. If an embroidered coat isn't your thing, stitch this motif on a bag, shirt, sandals, or pair of pants —let your creative instincts decide.

■ SIZE

Finished design: 2¾ × 3 inches (7.0 × 7.6 cm)

■ THREADS

100% cotton 6-strand embroidery threads (I used DMC Embroidery Floss, Article 117), 8.7 yards (8 m)/skein, 1 skein each of #471 very light avocado green, #815 medium garnet, #920 medium copper, #924 very dark gray green, and #3347 medium yellow green; 100% pearl cotton (I used DMC No. 8, Article 116), 88 yards (80 m) /ball, 1 (10 g) ball each of #471 very light avocado green, #815 medium garnet, #920 medium copper, and #3347 medium yellow green; 100% pearl cotton (I used DMC No. 5, Article 115), 27.3 yards (25 m)/skein, 1 skein of #924 very dark gray green

■ FABRIC

Item to be embellished: coat, shirt, bag

■ NOTIONS

Needles, chenille size 26 and embroidery size 8; embroidery hoop, 6 inches (15.2 cm) in diameter; fabric-marking pen or pencil
Optional: Lightweight nonwoven fusible interfacing, 5 × 5 inches (15.2 × 15.2 cm)

■ STITCHES

Couching, page 21
Satin stitch over double running stitch, page 30

■ INSTRUCTIONS

Note: Use the embroidery needle for the embroidery thread and the chenille needle for the No. 8 and No. 5 threads. Refer to the patterns for color placement.

Using one of the methods on pages 5–8, (I used an iron-transfer pencil), transfer the patterns to the inside of the item to be embroidered. If you're embellishing a coat, center the main motif on the back, with the top of the motif about 5 inches [12.7 cm] below the collar; place the small accent dots (right) along a back seam, on a pocket, or along the placket—you decide what looks best for your style of coat. Center and mount the design in the embroidery hoop. If the item to be embroidered is thinly woven, first trace the pattern to the piece of lightweight interfacing with the marking pen or pencil and trim within ¼ inch (6 mm) of the pattern; center and fuse to the inside of the item according to manufacturer's directions. Mount the item in the embroidery hoop with the wrong side facing up.

Accent dots

■ #920 medium copper

■ #924 very dark gray green

■ #3347 medium yellow green

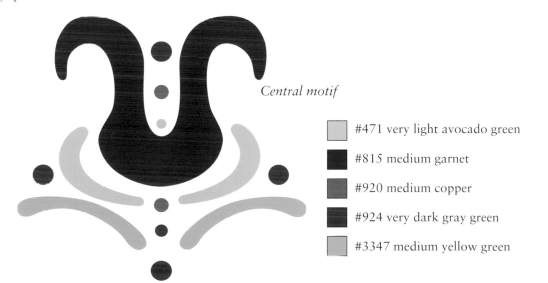

Central motif

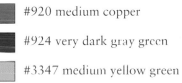

□ #471 very light avocado green

■ #815 medium garnet

■ #920 medium copper

■ #924 very dark gray green

■ #3347 medium yellow green

SATIN STITCH OVER DOUBLE RUNNING STITCH

Outline the area to be filled with double running stitch (page 20). Completely cover the motif area and outline stitches with satin stitches. Bring the needle up at 1, insert at 2, and bring up at 3. To further pad the satin stitches, add a row of chain stitches along the inside of the stitched outline before covering with satin stitches (see page 20). Note that the stitches shift direction with the curve in the pattern, always staying perpendicular to the outline of the design.

Outline all the shapes with running stitches and two strands of the embroidery thread. Remove the item from the hoop. Turn the item over and check the outline; use the marking pen to mark any outlines that need adjustment. Mount in the hoop with the right side of the item facing up. Using two strands of the embroidery thread and making fine adjustments as you go, stitch a second round of running stitches to create double running stitches.

Referring to the pattern for color placement, use the No. 8 or No. 5 thread in the chenille needle to cover the running stitches with vertical satin stitches or surface satin stitches (at right). For the main motif, the grain of the satin stitches should be perpendicular to the outline stitches as shown in illustration at left. Couch down the long threads of the main tulip motif with one strand of #815 embroidery thread.

Using one strand of the same color embroidery thread, couch down one strand of coordinating No. 8 or No. 5 thread around every shape, at the base of the satin stitches. Remove the item from the hoop. If desired, repeat part of the central motif on the front coat pocket flaps, omitting the main tulip motif and the dots that fill the tulip.

CHOOSING DURABLE STITCHES

Add stability and durability to your projects by choosing stitches that will withstand natural wear and tear. While you want to keep the back of your fabric free of bulky stitches, you also need to consider the effect of the stitches on the front of the fabric. Here are a few things to keep in mind:

• Stitches with long floats on the back and front of the fabric are susceptible to snagging and may loosen over time. If the item you are embroidering will be susceptible to heavy wear, choose stitches that are short and tight to the fabric.

• Consider using short-and-long satin stitches instead of regular satin stitches. Remember that any stitch with a long float is susceptible to snagging and may be couched down.

• If you are new to embroidery and have difficulty making tight French knots, try colonial knots (see page 35) instead.

• If you find it difficult to keep the loops of your chain stitches tight and uniform, use split stitches instead; the more strands you use, the more split stitch looks like chain stitch.

• If your stem, chain, split, or backstitches are loose, wrap them the way you do when you create a whipped stem stitch or a whipped backstitch (pages 24 and 89). To pull stitches tight to the fabric, cover with overcast stitches (page 21).

• Fewer threads will result in a fine surface with more stitches close to each other. As with woven fabric, increasing the number of the threads increases the durability and fineness of the surface.

AVOIDING BULK ON THE UNDERSIDE OF YOUR FABRIC

Conserve thread and avoid bulk on the back of fabric with surface satin stitch (see Figure 1). Satin stitch by bringing the needle up at 1, inserting at 2, and bringing the needle up at 3. Keep in mind that if you are working with light-weight fabrics it is easy to pull the stitch out between 2 and 3. To avoid pulling stitches out, use modified surface satin stitch (Figure 2). Bring the needle up at 1, down at 2, and skip one stitch width by bringing the needle up at 3. Insert at 4, bring the needle up at 5, and insert at 6 to fill the gap.

Be selective with stitches to conserve thread and reduce bulk on the back of the fabric. Here are a few tips:

• Choose a double running stitch over a backstitch; both give the same appearance on the front but backstitch has longer floats on the back that add bulk, and may become loose over time.

• For heavy-looking stitches on the right side of the fabric, try whipped backstitch or tightly whip a double running stitch instead of using an overcast stitch that pierces the fabric as it covers the foundation line of stitches.

• Take advantage of split, stem, and chain stitches—they all look like running stitches on the back of the fabric.

• If you notice that you're creating long floats on the back of the fabric when you move from one design element to another, consider whipping the working thread to the back of the previous stitches while moving to the area where the next stitches begin. For example, when you're stitching one of the ants from page 60, whip the working thread into the back of one leg, toward the body of the ant, before moving to the next leg.

• As you did while stitching the tulip portion of the central motif in this chapter, consider couching down long satin stitches and thick threads with a single strand of thread of the same color; the small anchoring stitches add texture and stability. This is important when using thick thread as the short floats created on the wrong side of the fabric are minimal in comparison to using a thick thread for couching.

• Using the waste knot technique will help you avoid knots on the back of the fabric; see page 27.

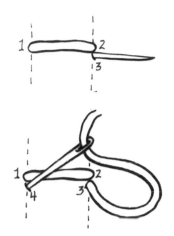

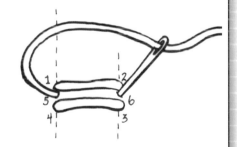

Figure 1. Surface satin stitch

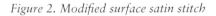

Figure 2. Modified surface satin stitch

TRENDY
HAIR TIES

These trendy hair ties are a great way
to use up small scraps of fabric and
experiment with color, all while tam-
ing your locks! You can dream up
other ways to play with them, too: Use
them as buttons on a coat, bag, shirt,
or pillow, or wear one as a brooch.
Check out the sidebar (page 36) if you
want to make a hair-tie tote for one
or all of the five embroidered covered
buttons featured in this chapter.

■ SIZES	■ THREADS	■ FABRIC	■ NOTIONS	■ STITCHES
Concentric circles: 1¼ inches (3.2 cm); Polka dots: 1⅛ inches (2.9 cm); Patchwork and Spiral: 1 inch (2.5 cm); Random knots: ⅞ inch (2.2 cm)	100% cotton 6-strand embroidery threads (I used DMC Embroidery Floss, Article 117), 8.7 yards (8 m) /skein, 1 skein each of the colors listed in the key	100% cotton: 8 × 8 inches (20.3 × 20.3 cm), 2 pieces of pale yellow, 2 pieces of red, and 1 piece of green	Half ball cover buttons, ¾ inch (1.9 cm), ⅝ inch (1.6 cm), and ⅞ inch (2.2 cm), 1 package each size, see notes below regarding quantities and type; needles, embroidery sizes 3 and 8; embroidery hoop, 6 inches (15.2 cm) in diameter; elastic hair ties, 5; acid-free craft glue	Colonial knots, page 35 Couching, page 21 French knots, page 21

For one-of-a-kind up-do's

■ INSTRUCTIONS

Note: Half ball cover buttons that are available as a kit (made by Dritz and other companies) come with tools for snapping the front and back button pieces together. If you're working with such a kit, do not use the white cup to hold the button top because it may crush the stitches. The blue plastic cup from the kit can be helpful when you're popping in the back bottom piece. If you are making only one button, refer to the individual instructions below for the size of button covers you should purchase.

Refer to the patterns, keys, and individual instructions on pages 34–35 for choosing fabric, thread colors, and color placement.

Using one of the transfer methods on pages 5–8, transfer one pattern to the center of each 8-inch (20.3-cm) piece of fabric. Your pattern lines will be completely covered so feel free to use permanent transfer marks like those created by most graphite pencils and iron-transfer pens and pencils. Mount the fabric in the embroidery hoop before stitching; remove the fabric when stitching is complete. Stitch the patterns according to the directions listed with the individual patterns.

■ CONCENTRIC CIRCLES

Working on the red fabric, use colonial knots, the size 8 needle, and three strands of thread to complete the design. Use a ⅞-inch (2.2-cm) button cover for the finishing instructions on page 37.

■ PATCHWORK

Working on the red fabric, use colonial knots, the size 8 needle, and three strands of thread to complete the design. Use a ¾-inch (1.9-cm) button cover for the finishing instructions on page 37.

■ POLKA DOTS

Working on the green fabric from the center out, use the size 3 needle to bring up four strands of the color to be couched and couch down with one strand of contrasting thread in the size 8 needle. The colors listed in the key indicate the four strands of the couched thread. Change the colors of the single-strand couching thread at random, using the colors listed in the key and, if desired, #676 and #3051. Use a ⅞-inch (2.2-cm) button cover for the finishing instructions on page 37.

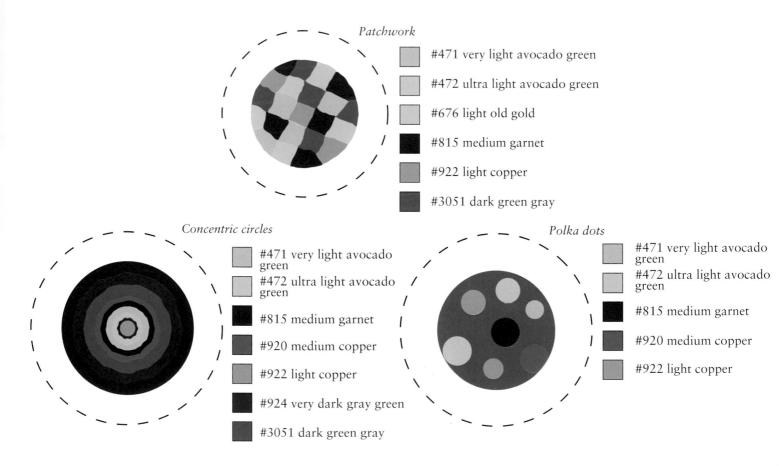

Patchwork

#471 very light avocado green

#472 ultra light avocado green

#676 light old gold

#815 medium garnet

#922 light copper

#3051 dark green gray

Concentric circles

#471 very light avocado green

#472 ultra light avocado green

#815 medium garnet

#920 medium copper

#922 light copper

#924 very dark gray green

#3051 dark green gray

Polka dots

#471 very light avocado green

#472 ultra light avocado green

#815 medium garnet

#920 medium copper

#922 light copper

■ SPIRAL

Working on the pale yellow fabric, bring up one strand of #471 in the size 8 needle in the center of the fabric; park the needle in the fabric near the edge of the hoop. Bring up six strands of #815 in the size 3 needle in the center of the fabric; remove the needle. Bring up six strands of #472 in the size 3 needle; remove the needle. Using #471 in the size 8 needle, couch down #815 and #472 from the center out in a circular pattern, alternating the couched colors to completely cover the design in a spiral. When you've covered the design, use the size 3 needle to independently take the six-stranded threads to the back. For tips on handling long strands of couched thread, see page 80. Use a ¾-inch (1.9-cm) button cover for the finishing instructions on page 37.

■ RANDOM KNOTS

Working on the pale yellow fabric, use three strands of thread in the size 3 needle to randomly fill the circle with French knots. In making the blended needles listed in the key, use one strand of each color. Use a ⅝-inch (1.6-cm) button cover for the finishing instructions on page 37; this design is shown on the bag on page 36.

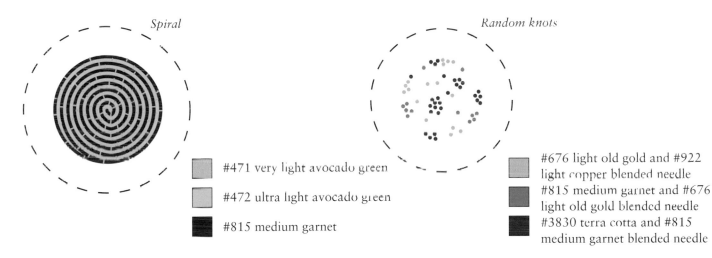

Spiral

Random knots

■ #471 very light avocado green

■ #472 ultra light avocado green

■ #815 medium garnet

■ #676 light old gold and #922 light copper blended needle

■ #815 medium garnet and #676 light old gold blended needle

■ #3830 terra cotta and #815 medium garnet blended needle

COLONIAL KNOTS

Bring the needle up at 1 and make a figure 8 with the thread around the needle according to the illustration. Insert near 1 while holding the thread taut at the base of the knot while you pull the needle and thread through the knot and fabric.

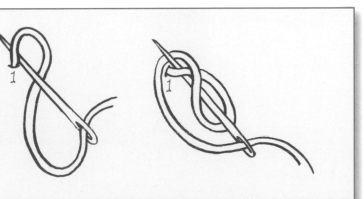

35

QUICK AND EASY HAIR-TIE TOTE

There are lots of ways to incorporate embellished buttons around your home: Update old coats, skirts, and shirts by replacing plain or mismatched buttons, use one as a zipper pull, wear one as a brooch by removing the button's shank and gluing a pin back to the back, string several on a thin bracelet. Or, you can make a little tote for your hair ties; and adorn it with a button!

To make the tote, you will need one square of fabric for the front and one for the lining (I used 6½-inch [16.5-cm] squares, which resulted in a 4-inch [10.2-cm] square tote), one snap, sewing thread, size 10 embroidery needle, a decorative covered button, and a sewing machine (optional). With right sides facing and using a ½-inch (1.3-cm) seam allowance, join the two squares by machine stitching (or hand stitching with tightly spaced double running stitches), leaving a 2-inch (5.1-cm) opening in the center of one side. Trim the seam allowances to ¼ inch (6 mm), trim the corners to ⅛ inch (3 mm), and turn right sides out. Push the corners out with a knitting needle or chopstick and press. Slip-stitch (page 105) the opening closed.

Fold three of the corners to the center with the lining side facing and use slip stitch to join the two sides of the bottom flap with the adjacent edges of the two side flaps. Stitch the button to the right side of the tip of the unfolded fourth corner and stitch one of the snap parts to the lining, directly under the button. Fold this last corner ⅛ inch (3 mm) over the three joined flaps and mark where the snap lies on the fabric; stitch the second snap part to the tote. Simply increase or decrease the dimensions of the fabric squares to make a tote or bag of any size. Feel free to experiment with fabrics; I pieced the right side of my tote before joining the front to the lining.

■ FINISHING

When stitching is complete, remove the fabric from the hoop and trim the fabric along the outside-line of the pattern. Assemble the covered button with the button size listed with the stitching directions. Run a light line of glue along the inside edge of the button top. Allow the glue to dry for about two minutes. Center the button top over the back of the embroidery with the embroidery face down, on a hard surface covered with a terry towel. Tightly pull the edges of the fabric toward the inside of the button top and tuck the edges into the glue. Snap the back of the button into the top with your hands or, if available, with the aid of the blue plastic cup from the kit.

After the glue is dry, create a hair tie by folding one end of an elastic hair tie in half and threading it through the shank of the button. Pull the folded end through the loop created on the opposite end. If you have trouble pulling the elastic hair tie through the button shank, thread the elastic hair tie with a scrap piece of thread and tightly pull the ends of the thread through the shank until one end of the elastic hair tie is also through the shank; pull this end through the loop created on the opposite end. Repeat finishing instructions for the four other embroidered pieces of fabric.

Mix and match for even more fun

Preserve special memories in an unexpected way

Curtain fabric
for kitchen
windows
100% cotton
2002
Ft. Collins, CO
Melinda Barta

Quilt border
100% cotton
1978
Evergreen, CO
Katherine
Sabiton

Pillow fabric
for a friend
100% cotton
1990
Ault, CO
Ellie Baker

Patch for
shirt sleeve
100% cotton
1980s
Omaha, NE
Worn by
Sarah Helm

FAMILY TREE TEXTILE
SCRAPBOOK

Instead of keeping family heirloom textiles tucked away in a
dark closet, bring them out for all to see. Store your cherished
trimmings, findings, and edgings in a scrapbook you make for
recording textiles. It's a fun, rewarding way for your family to
share and document its history in the world of fiber!

■ SIZE

8½ × 10 inches (21.6 × 25.4 cm)

■ THREADS

100% cotton 6-strand embroidery threads, 1 skein each of two colors of your choice (I used DMC Embroidery Floss, Article 117) 8.7 yards (8 m)/skein, 1 skein each of #221 very dark shell pink and #838 very dark beige brown; quilting thread, color to match the pages of your scrapbook (I used cream)

■ FABRIC

Collection of your favorite antique or contemporary fabric scraps, handkerchiefs, edgings, trimmings, findings, patterns, and buttons

■ NOTIONS

Needle, embroidery size 7; scrapbook with a removable spine and acid-free pages (I used a Kolo photograph album, Newbury, sage, 8½ × 10 [21.6 × 25.4 cm], with a 2½ inch [6.4-cm] square window); acid-free adhesive; colored paper and vellum, 11 × 8½ inches (27.9 × 21.6 cm), 1 sheet each
Optional: Vellum and organza envelopes

■ STITCHES

Knot stitch edging, page 41
Running stitch, page 20

■ INSTRUCTIONS

There are a few basic elements that guide you in the creation of your fabric scrapbook:

Check scrapbooking supply and craft stores for a variety of archival-quality decorations and envelopes. Organza envelopes are ideal for storing fabric scraps and buttons. To secure the envelopes to the pages of the book, use quilting thread and a running stitch along the base of the top flap of the envelope. To display your favorite buttons, stitch a few to the envelope and the paper. To prevent the buttons from warping the book, use buttons without shanks.

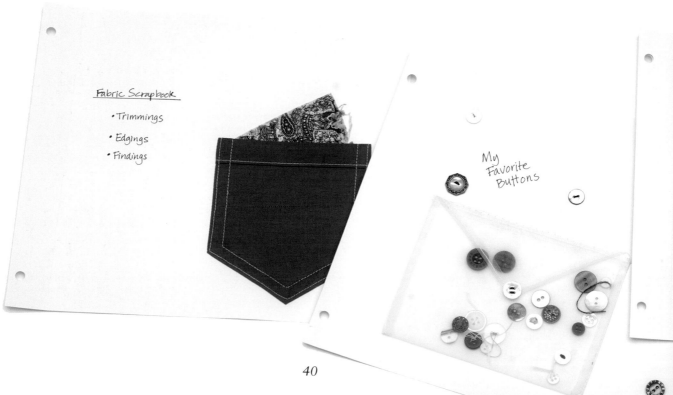

My scrapbook has an open window in the cover where I keep one of my favorite scraps. To further personalize the journal, stitch a monogram from pages 114–115 for the window.

The scrapbook's removable spine makes it easy to extract pages for stitching, and it accommodates added thickness. If a ribbon holds your scrapbook together, feel free to change the color of the ribbon; for added interest, use an embroidered ribbon (see page 48).

To keep the edges of your favorite scraps from fraying, consider trimming and embroidering the edges. I trimmed mine to 2½ inches (6.4 cm) square and used a size 7 embroidery needle to secure the edges with four strands of either #221 or #838 and knot stitch edging. Adhere fabric scraps to the pages of the book with acid-free adhesive and label each scrap with information about its origin, former owner (if any), and date. If you would like to make a detailed logbook, add fiber content information, photographs, places the fabric was used, a list of all former owners, where and when the fabric was purchased or made, and the embellishment and construction techniques.

my favorite patterns

KNOT STITCH EDGING
Working from left to right on the edge of the fabric, bring the needle up from the back, ⅛ inch (3 mm) from the edge and make a blanket stitch (page 89). Before moving to the next blanket stitch, loop the needle behind the two threads that hang from the edge of the fabric. To keep even tension, you may find it helpful to pinch the top of the blanket stitch while you make the knot. Repeat as with blanket stitch, inserting the needle into the right side of the fabric and taking the next stitch about ¼ inch (6 mm) to the right of the previous stitch.

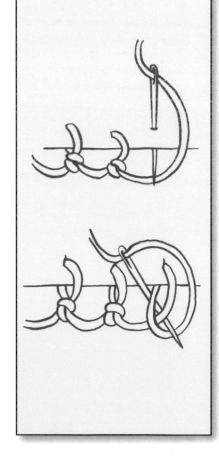

HOW TO SEW A POCKET

Knowing how to make a pocket is a valuable skill. Instead of stitching it to a coat, embellishing a bag, or repairing a shirt or blue jeans, use it to store trimmings and fragments in your scrapbook.

Transfer all the lines of the pocket pattern to a 7-inch (17.8-cm) square piece of fabric using one of the transfer methods on pages 5–8. Cut the fabric along the outside line. Fold over the top edge at the purple dashed line with right sides facing and press. Fold again along the red dashed line and press. Machine stitch (or use tightly spaced double running or backstitches) the fold created at the purple line to the body of the pocket within $\frac{1}{16}$ inch (1.5 mm) of the edge of the inside fold line. Fold the side and bottom edges back along the blue dashed lines and press. If you're sewing the pocket to a second piece of fabric, pin the pocket in place on the right side of the fabric. Stitch $\frac{1}{16}$ inch (1.5 mm) from the outer edges around the sides and bottom of the pocket. Stitch around the outer edges again, ¼ inch (6 mm) from the previously stitched line.

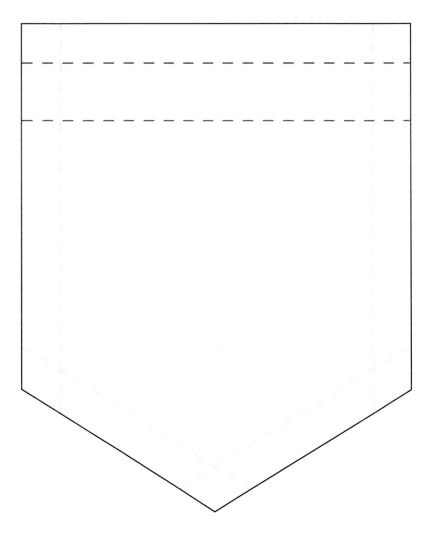

Enlarge pattern by 125%

42

Vellum envelopes are a great way to store fragile scraps; they allow the fabric to be seen without having to remove the pieces from the envelope. The set of envelopes I purchased came with cards, which I used as tags to label the fragments. These envelopes are also great for storing old patterns and charts.

By using running stitches to attach to paper an embroidered handkerchief I received from my grandmother, I have made its future safe from plastics, moisture, and damaging sunlight.

Vellum envelopes let you see your treasures

COZY CREWEL
MITTENS

Crewel embroidery is traditionally defined by
the use of lightly twisted, two-ply, worsted
wool embroidery threads on a linen or cotton
twill ground. Here, worsted wool fabric is
used as the background for an elegant,
old-fashioned, embroidered thistle, stitched
in wool and wool/silk threads. If you are
looking for a quick addition to your
fall and winter outfits, sew the fabric
into mittens after you have
embroidered the thistle, or part
of the stem and a couple of
leaves as shown on the left
mitten. Add novelty yarn
around the wrists in a bright
color for more verve!

■ SIZE	■ THREADS	■ FABRIC	■ NOTIONS	■ STITCHES
Finished design: 2 × 3 inches (5.1 × 7.6 cm) Mittens: 10 × 6 inches (25.4 × 15.2 cm)	100% wool embroidery threads (I used DMC Medicis Wool, Article 475), single-strand two-ply thread, 27.3 yards (25 m)/skein, 1 skein each of ecru, #8411 moss green, and #8932 light blue; 50% silk/50% wool threads (I used Caron Collection Impressions), single-strand variegated thread, 36 yards (33 m)/skein, 1 skein of #085 antique brass; decorative yarn for mitten edge (I used Crystal Palace Fizz, 100% polyester), 120 yards (110 m/ball, 1 ball, variegated green); sewing thread, maroon and green	Worsted wool: 100% wool, maroon, 14 × 9 inches (35.6 × 22.9 cm), 4 pieces	Needles, chenille size 22 and a sharp size 7; embroidery hoop, 6 inches (15.2 cm) in diameter; pins Optional: sewing machine	Chain stitch, page 21 Couching, page 21 French knots, page 21 Stem stitch, page 21 Lattice pattern filling stitch, page 47 Whipstitch, page 103

■ INSTRUCTIONS

Note: The mitten pattern is for a size medium mitten, 4½ inches (10.8 cm) across the top of the knuckles. Reduce or enlarge the pattern for a size small or large mitten so that the measurement across the knuckles is either ¼ inch (6 mm) smaller or larger than the mitten pattern. Use the chenille needle unless otherwise noted.

Using one of the transfer methods on pages 5–8, center and transfer the mitten pattern to the right side of one piece of wool. Center and transfer a mirror image of the mitten pattern to the right side of another piece of wool, omitting part of the motif if desired (as I did on my left mitten). I recommend using the tissue paper transfer method on page 8 and the green sewing thread for basting; doing so makes it easy to transfer the mirror image to the left mitten because the paper is transparent. Regardless of the transfer method used, baste along the solid outside line.

■ EMBROIDERING THE MITTENS

Mount one piece of fabric with the transferred motif in the embroidery hoop. Refer to Figure 1 (page 47) for color placement and see the sidebar on page 46 if you need help determining the difference between plies and strands. Stem-stitch the leaf outline and stem of A with two strands of #8411. Use one strand for all other stitches: Stem stitch B to the right of the previous line with #085. Using #085, fill petal C with chain stitches that are worked from the outside inward. Stem stitch the remaining lines indicated by D with #8411. Outline the thistle indicated by E with #8932. Chain-stitch lines F with #8932 and lines G with ecru just inside the thistle flower and bud outlines. Fill petal H with lattice filling stitch: Use #085 for the latticework foundation and tack down the intersections with #8411. Fill petal I with lattice filling stitch: Use #8932 for the latticework foundation and tack down the intersections with ecru. Stitch all French knots (J) with ecru. Remove the fabric from the hoop. If you used the

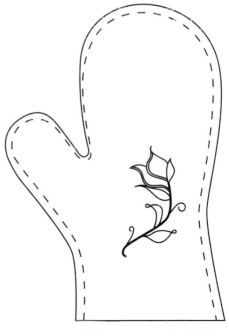

Enlarge pattern by 336%.

WORKING WITH WOOL THREADS

There are just a few tips to guide you when working with wool threads:

• Do not try to thread the needle straight on as you do with cotton or silk. Instead, use a needle threader or fold the top inch (2.5 cm) over the needle and pull the thread tails as you move your fingers toward the eye of the needle to pinch the thread (Figure 1). Remove the needle and with the tip of the folded portion between your fingers, thread the needle (Figure 2).

• All crewel wool threads are by definition two-ply, not to be confused with two-stranded, and the plies should not be separated. When a project calls for two strands, use two lengths of the two-ply crewel wool to give you a total of four plies.

• Always use needles with long eyes, such as tapestry, chenille, and large embroidery (crewel) needles. Doing so will make it easier to thread the needle and prevent the yarns from fraying.

• Cut strands a little shorter than usual. Working with strands that are no longer than 15 inches (38.1 cm) will prevent fraying and preserve the loft in the yarn by reducing the number of times the thread is pulled through the fabric.

• Avoid tying knots at the end of the thread. The knots will turn out smaller than predicted. Instead, use the waste knot technique or any of the other methods for hiding knots and thread tails on page 27.

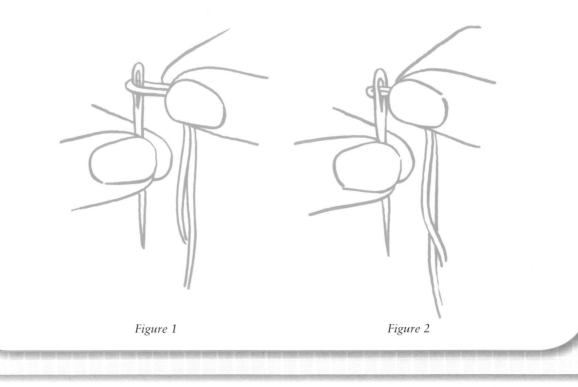

Figure 1   *Figure 2*

tissue transfer method for the thistle motif, remove the basting stitches that indicate the thistle from the wrong side. Repeat for the other piece of wool with the transferred motif.

◼ CONSTRUCTING THE MITTENS

Pin one of the embroidered fabric pieces to one of the nonembroidered pieces with right sides facing; repeat for the second embroidered piece and the last piece of fabric, making sure pins are placed inside the basted outline. Cut along the outside basted line; you will now have both the front and back mitten pieces cut out. Repeat for the second set of pinned fabric layers. Zigzag stitch with a machine, or blanket stitch (page 89) by hand, along the cuff edges of the four mitten pieces to keep the raw edges from fraying. Referring to the dashed lines of the pattern (page 45) for placement, join one set of mitten pieces by machine stitching (or using tightly spaced double running or backstitches); note where the seam allowance narrows between the index finger and thumb and sew this area twice for reinforcement. Remove the pins. Trim the seam allowances to ⅛ inch (3 mm) and machine or hand stitch the raw edges with maroon sewing thread: For sewing by machine, set the zigzag stitches to match the width of the seam allowances; if you prefer hand stitching, cover the seam allowances with blanket stitch. Turn the mitten right-side out. With the green sewing thread and the sharp needle, couch the novelty yarn around the cuff, ½ inch (1.3 cm) from the raw edges. Fold the cuffs to the inside ¼ inch (6 mm) and secure with a whipstitch and maroon sewing thread. Repeat construction directions for the remaining mitten pieces.

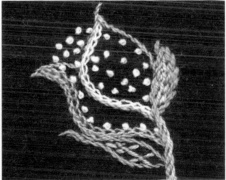

□ ecru

□ #085 antique brass

□ #8411 moss green

□ #8932 light blue

Figure 1

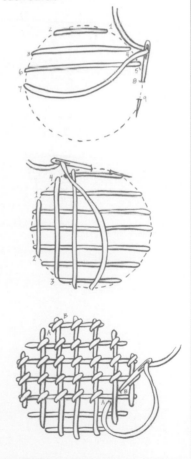

RICH VELVET

RIBBONS
AND A RADIANT BEADED
BAG

Decorative, economical, and—best of all—reusable, these richly textured velvet ribbons are perfect for adorning special gifts, notebooks, and boxes. Backing them with silk ribbons, as instructed in the sidebar, hides thread tails and adds a splash of color. Another great idea is to personalize ribbons with embroidery, then whipstitch them to the hem of your jeans, coat, or skirt, and in minutes you've transformed your wardrobe. Try your hand at bead embroidery and make a little beaded bag with coordinating motifs.

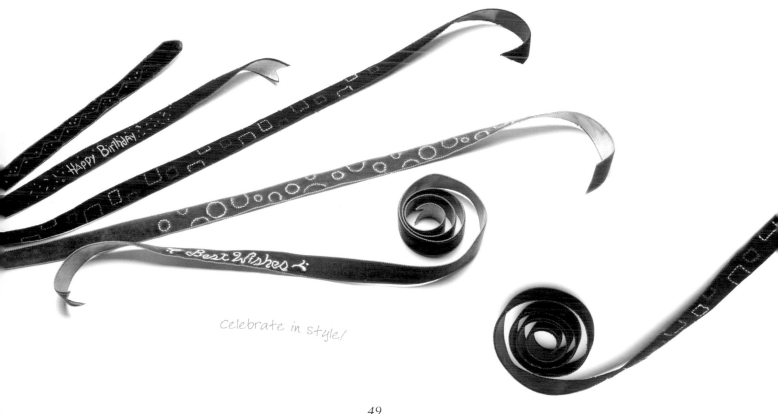

Celebrate in style!

■ SIZE

Ribbons:
½ × 24
inches (1.3
× 61.0 cm)
Bag: 5¼
× 6 inches
(13.3 ×
15.2 cm)

■ THREADS

100% cotton 6-strand
embroidery threads (I used
DMC Embroidery Floss,
Article 117), 8.7 yards
(8 m)/skein, 1 skein each of
ecru and #3364 pine green;
100% silk 6-stranded
thread (I used Pearsall's
Filoselle Embroidery Silk),
1 skein each of the colors
listed in the keys

■ FABRIC

Velvet ribbons:
½ × 24 inches
(1.3 x 61.0 cm)
each of teal,
red, green, pur-
ple, and maroon

■ NOTIONS

Needle, embroidery
size 9; inner ring of
an embroidery hoop
wrapped in fabric (see
page 9 if you need to
wrap your hoop), 6
inches (15.2 cm) in
diameter; appliqué or
other small pins, ½
inch (1.3 cm) long

■ STITCHES

Backstitch, page 20
Double running stitch,
page 20
French knots, page 21
Herringbone stitch,
page 57
Satin over double run-
ning stitch, page 30
Stem stitch, page 21
Whipped stem stitch,
page 24

■ INSTRUCTIONS

Transfer the patterns to the ribbons by using one of the transfer methods on pages 5–8. (I used a one-step transfer pen to
make a faint outline of the patterns and drew over these marks
with a white fabric-marking pen.) The tissue paper transfer
method is also great for velvet; see page 8. Note that the Circles
and Squares and Rectangles patterns are just one portion of the
design; repeat the patterns on either side as desired. When you're using two
strands of silk, run the thread lightly through a thread conditioner like Thread
Heaven, if necessary (see Working with Silk and Wire, page 73). To avoid crushing
the velvet, stretch one ribbon across the inner ring of the embroidery hoop, pin to
the fabric of the hoop along the outside edges, and remove the pins when stitching
is complete. Use the embroidery needle for all stitches and refer to the patterns for
color placement.

■ CIRCLES

Backstitch the circles with two strands of silk on the green ribbon.

	#313 ecru
	#095 maize gold
	#158 dull blue
	#253 willow green

■ SQUARES AND RECTANGLES

Backstitch the squares and rectangles with two strands of silk on the maroon ribbon.

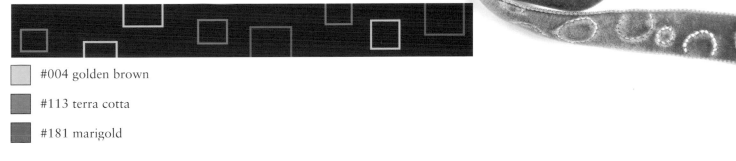

■ #004 golden brown

■ #113 terra cotta

■ #181 marigold

■ HAPPY BIRTHDAY

Working on the red ribbon, stitch the text with stem stitch and one strand of #3364 cotton thread; tightly whipstitch to cover the stem stitches with one strand of #014 silk. Use one strand of silk to stitch the confetti with whipped stem stitch and French knots.

■ #004 golden brown

■ #014 apple green

■ #256 willow green

■ #340 charcoal

Everyone loves velvet ribbons

■ **BEST WISHES**

Working on the teal ribbon with one strand of ecru cotton thread, stem stitch the text and outline the scrolls with double running stitch. With one strand of #313 silk, tightly whip and cover the stem stitches of the text, cover the double running stitches of the outlined side scrolls with satin stitch, and make French knots where indicated by dots on the pattern.

 #313 ecru

■ **PURPLE ABSTRACT**

Working on the purple ribbon with two strands of #066 silk thread, use herringbone stitch to work the red lines indicated on the pattern. Using the same color, work back along the red lines with one strand of thread and tack down the diagonal lines of the herringbone stitches with two evenly spaced stitches. Make French knots with one strand #132 silk where indicated by the dots on the pattern.

 #066 crimson

#132 goblin green

BACKING YOUR EMBROIDERIES: MAKING REVERSIBLE RIBBONS

Covering the thread tails and stitches on the back of your embroideries will prevent pulled stitches. To cover the back of the ribbons and make them reversible, you will need four 24-inch (61.0-cm) pieces of ½-inch (1.3-cm) wide nonwoven fusible web and four 24-inch (61.0-cm) pieces of ½-inch (1.3 cm) wide hand-dyed silk ribbon (I used one piece each of YLI #012 green and two each of pieces of #010 green/tan and #001 red to back the ribbons in this chapter).

After completing stitching, trim the thread tails and lay one ribbon right side down on a white terry-cloth towel. (Although it is best to press velvet on a pin board designed for pressing velvet, the low nap of these ribbons will not be damaged if they're pressed on a towel.) Lay one 24-inch (61.0-cm) piece of fusible web on the back of the embroidered ribbon and cover with one 24-inch (61.0-cm) piece of silk ribbon. (I fused the #012 green silk ribbon to the back of the Best Wishes embroidery, the #001 red silk ribbon to the back of the Purple Abstract and Squares and Rectangles embroideries, the #010 green/tan silk ribbon to the back of the Happy Birthday and Circles embroideries.) Press on a low setting to fuse one coordinating silk ribbon to the back of one embroidered ribbon and trim the ends of the ribbon at a 45-degree angle. Repeat fusing for the other ribbons, but keep in mind that you do not need to back the embroidered ribbons with silk if you are going to mount them to objects like boxes, photograph albums, or clothing. Use the same method to back other embroideries, but use medium-weight nonwoven fusible web and the backing fabric of your choice.

Dream up your own design

A RADIANT BEADED BAG

This project shows the versatility of the motifs presented earlier in this chapter. Use your favorite patterns—I designed this bag with the Circles ribbon pattern for the body of the bag and the Squares and Rectangles ribbon pattern for the top edge of the bag, and I bordered the top and bottom of each of the patterns with a row of beads. To make the bag you will need one 10- × 7-inch (25.4- × 17.8-cm) piece of heavy-weight fabric (I used an orange placemat) for the body, one 14- × 7-inch (35.6- × 17.8-cm) piece of medium-weight fabric (I used a lime green napkin) for the lining, two 36- × 1¾-inch (91.4- × 4.5-cm) pieces of medium-weight fabric (I used light teal cotton fabric and a pieced-together orange napkin) for the strap, a sewing machine (optional), a size 11 short (also referred to as a beading sharp) beading needle, a size 9 embroidery needle, white beading thread (I used size A Silamide Waxed Nylon Beadstring), sewing thread to match the lining fabric, and two colors of size 11° seed beads (I used matte-finish, foil-lined, lime green and teal Japanese seed beads).

See the Bead Embroidery 101 sidebar (page 56) for tips on transferring patterns and stabilizing designs. Using one of the transfer methods on pages 5–8, transfer two 6-inch (15.2-cm) long segments of the Circles ribbon pattern to the right side of the body fabric with the patterns parallel to the short end of the fabric and the patterns centered side by side: Place the top line of one pattern 1¼ inches (3.2 cm) below one short end of the body fabric and the top line of the second pattern 1 inch (2.5 cm) below the bottom line of the first transferred pattern. Transfer one 6-inch (15.2-cm) long segment of the Squares and Rectangles ribbon pattern to the right side of the lining fabric with the pattern parallel to one short end of the fabric, centered side by side, and with the bottom line of the pattern ¾ inch (1.9 cm) from one short end.

Using the beading needle, beading thread, and alternating between the bead colors of your choice, backstitch the circles, squares, and rectangles; refer to the backstitch with beads illustration on page 57, if needed. Couch down a row of beads in the color of your choice for the top and bottom borders of the patterns.

Fold the body fabric in half, matching the short ends and with right sides together; press. Using a ½-inch (1.3-cm) seam allowance, stitch the side seams together with the sewing thread by machine stitching (or hand stitching with tightly spaced double running or backstitches); use a zipper foot to bypass the beads, if machine stitching. Repeat folding and stitching for the lining fabric. Trim the seam allowances of both the lining and body fabrics to ¼ inch (6 mm); trim the corners. Turn the body right side out and push the corners out with a knitting needle or chopstick. With wrong sides facing, turn the top edge of the lining fabric over ½ inch (1.3 cm) and press; turn over another 1 inch (2.5 cm) and press again. Insert the lining fabric inside the body fabric, tucking the top raw edges of the body fabric in the fold of the lining fabric. Use the sewing thread and embroidery needle to slip-stitch (page 105) the bottom folded edge of the lining to the body fabric.

To make the strap, join the long sides of the two 36- × 1¾-inch (91.4- × 4.5-cm) pieces of medium-weight fabric with right sides facing and using a ¼-inch (6-mm) seam allowance. Turn the strap right sides out (I placed a safety pin in one layer of fabric near the end and threaded the safety pin through the tube of fabric); press. With right sides facing, press back the last ¼ inch (6 mm) of each end. With the raw folded ends of the strap facing the lining, pin each end inside the bag, centered over the side seams with the ends of the strap 1 inch (2.5 cm) below the top edge. Slip-stitch the strap to the lining fabric around the edges of the strap that touch the lining with the sewing thread and embroidery needle; a few slip stitches should be deep enough to catch the wrong side of the body fabric.

BEAD EMBROIDERY 101

• The tissue paper transfer method (see page 8) is a great way to transfer designs for bead embroidery. However, substituting paper for tissue paper and applying a mirror image of your pattern to the back of the fabric (instead of the front as when you're using tissue paper) will add stability to your work and help control the tension of your thread. Simply baste the edges of a photocopy of your pattern to the wrong side of the fabric, baste the design lines through the paper, turn the fabric over and, without removing the paper pattern, bead over the basted design lines. If the item you beaded will be washed, remove the paper when stitching is complete by lightly wetting the paper before tearing it off. When using paper on the back of your work you will not need to use an embroidery hoop. The interfacing transfer method (see page 7) is also great for bead embroidery; however, you will need to work on the right side of the fabric (instead of the back as when you're using the interfacing transfer method), and will need to baste the design lines to make them visible on the right side of the fabric before beading.

• As when stringing beads for a necklace, bag handle, or bracelet, it is always best to reinforce your work by passing back through the beads at least one more time. When working shapes with tight curves and long lines (like the circles and borderlines in this chapter); the additional passes of thread will do more than strengthen the stitches—they will help smooth the shapes and straighten lines.

• Beading needles are available in a variety of sizes (10 through 13 and 15 through 16) and most are available in two lengths—short and long. As a general rule, a size 15 needle is suitable for a size 15° seed bead, a size 11 needle is suitable for a size 11° seed bead, and so on. There are exceptions: If your beads are foil-lined or the holes are just too small, you may have to use a thinner needle. As with most needles, the larger the number, the thinner and shorter the needle. Although the small eye of beading sharp needles is sometimes hard to thread, beading sharp needles are advantageous because of their strength.

For more tips on bead embroidery see *Beaded Embellishment: Techniques and Designs for Embroidering on Cloth* by Amy C. Clarke and Robin Atkins (Interweave Press, 2002).

HERRINGBONE STITCH

Baste, using long temporary running stitches, or draw two parallel lines to mark the top and bottom lines of the area to be covered. Working from left to right and bottom to top, bring the needle up at 1 and insert at 2. Bring the needle up at 3, $\frac{1}{8}$ to $\frac{1}{4}$ inch (3 to 6 mm) to the left of 2. Insert the needle at 4 and bring up at 5, overlapping the previously stitched lines to create small Xs at the top and bottom of the row.

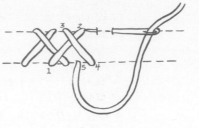

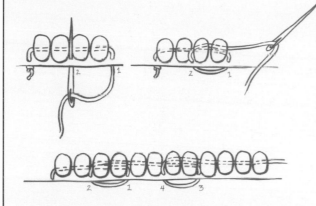

BACKSTITCH WITH BEADS

Bring the needle up on the left end of the line you want to cover, string on four beads, and while holding the beads against the fabric, insert the needle into the fabric at the end of the line of beads. Bring the needle up at 2 (between the second and third bead), and pass through the last two beads. Repeat by picking up four more beads; insert the needle at 3 and bring the needle up at 4. To make sure that the beads lie flat without gaps between them—the distance between the starting point and 1 should be equal to the space occupied by four beads; the distance between 2 and 3 should be equal to the space occupied by six beads.

COUCHING WITH BEADS

Bring the needle up on the left end of the line you want to cover and string on the number of beads required to cover the entire line; park the needle at the end of the line, perpendicular to the line. Pull the thread taut to straighten the beads over the line and secure the thread by making a figure 8 around the needle. With a second needle and thread, start three beads beyond the start of the line and couch down the thread strung with beads after every third bead—make sure to come up precisely between two beads. When you have reached the end of the line, bring both needles and threads to the back and knot.

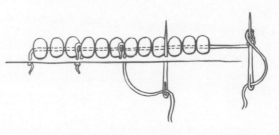

BIB

Many mothers and fathers are hesitant to dress their babies with crisp, clean hand-embroidered bibs because they know the bibs will rarely stay that way for long! I designed the Antsy Baby Bib so that food stains look natural among the ants scurrying around for crumbs. And instead of starting with a new bib, update a used one. If you want to shorten your stitching time, see the sidebar (page 62) for instructions on how to stamp the ants' bodies with fabric paint so you have only the legs and antennae to stitch.

■ SIZE	■ THREADS	■ FABRIC	■ NOTIONS	■ STITCHES
6¾ × 7¼ inches (17.1 × 18.4 cm); not including ties	100% cotton 6-strand embroidery threads (I used DMC Embroidery Floss, Article 117), 8.7 yards (8 m)/ skein, 1 skein each of the colors listed in the key and blanc	Baby bib, 100% cotton, white, about 6¾ × 7¼ inches (17.1 × 18.4 cm)	Needle, embroidery size 9; embroidery hoop, 5 inches (12.7 cm) in diameter	Backstitch, page 20 French knots, page 21 Long-and-short satin stitch, page 20 One-sided fern stitch, page 63 Overcast stitch, page 21 Satin over double running stitch, page 30 Seed stitch, page 20 Straight stitch, page 20

■ INSTRUCTIONS

Note: Be careful not to pull the stitches so tight that they distort the fabric. Unless otherwise noted, use two strands of thread for all stitches and refer to the pattern for color placement. Using one of the transfer methods on pages 5–8, transfer the motifs to the bib. Mount the bib in the embroidery hoop.

■ ANTS

Outline the ant bodies in double running stitch with #310 and fill the bodies with vertical satin stitches to cover the double running stitches. Indicate the legs with backstitch. For the lone red ant, use #815 for its last body segment. Use one strand of blanc and short, straight stitches to create highlights on the middle body segment and head. Use straight stitch for the antennae.

■ LADYBUG

Use double running stitch to outline the body and head and to divide the center of the body vertically. Outline the dots on the back with #310 and double running stitch; fill with vertical satin stitches to cover the double running stitches. Stitch the background of the body with #815 by covering the running stitches with satin stitches: Start at the center and angle stitches out toward the head at a 45-degree angle. Using #310, stitch the head with vertical satin stitches, backstitch the legs, indicate the antennae with short straight stitches, and top each antenna with a French knot. Use one strand of blanc and short, straight stitches to create highlights on the head and body.

■ GRASSHOPPER

Outline all areas with double running stitches and #471. Note that the upper segment of the hind leg is divided into two areas, A and C. Work A and B with #472 and satin stitches that run parallel to the outlines; add highlights with short, straight stitches and one strand of #310 and one strand of #704. Work C with satin stitches that are perpendicular to the outlines; add highlights with short, straight stitches and one strand of #310. Stitch D (forelegs, middle leg, and antennae) with overcast stitch and a blended needle made of one strand each of #472 and #704. Use vertical satin stitches to fill E (the abdomen and area under the thorax) with two strands of #3346; add highlights with short, straight stitches and one strand of #3051. Use #704 and satin stitch to fill F (the head) with stitches that start from the top of the head and angle toward the mouth. Stitch the eye with satin stitch and #310. Use satin stitch to fill G (the thorax) with stitches that start at the top and angle toward the middle leg. Stitch H (the wing) with long-and-short satin stitch and #704; add highlights with short, straight stitches and one strand of #327. Remove the bib from the hoop.

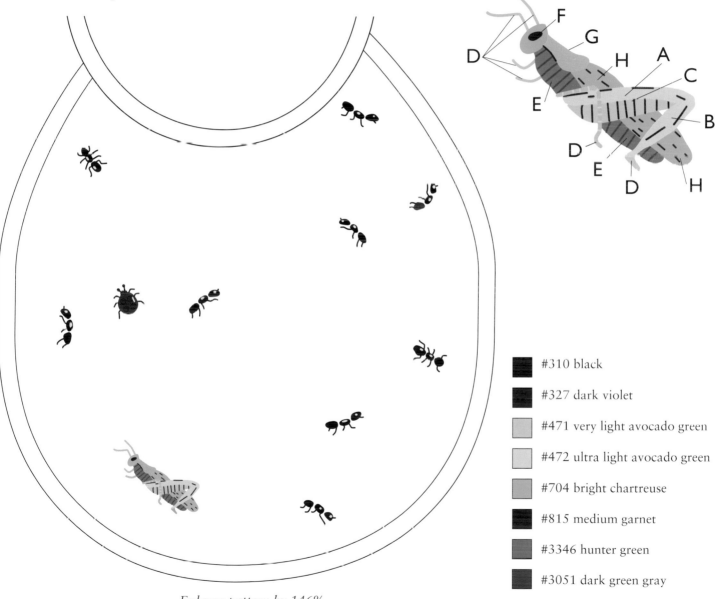

#310 black

#327 dark violet

#471 very light avocado green

#472 ultra light avocado green

#704 bright chartreuse

#815 medium garnet

#3346 hunter green

#3051 dark green gray

Enlarge pattern by 146%

61

FABRIC STAMPING 101

Save time stitching by stamping the ant bodies with your own carved stamps. To make the stamps, you will need a white eraser cut to ½ × 1 × ½ inches (1.3 × 2.5 × 1.3 cm), one small bottle of black craft fabric paint (available at craft stores), a scrap piece of cardboard, an X-acto knife, and a paintbrush.

Draw over the three body segments of one of the ants from the pattern with a pencil. Center and press the ½-inch (1.3-cm) square end of the eraser onto the ant—the pencil marks will naturally transfer the reverse image to the eraser. Hold the X-acto knife vertically and cut ⅛ inch (3 mm) into the eraser around the pencil marks. Holding the knife horizontally, carefully cut into the eraser toward the vertical cuts to carve away the background material. Make sure you control the depth of the knife so you don't accidentally cut away the body segments. If necessary, smooth by trimming the edges of the segments with the knife after removing all the background material.

Spread a thin layer of fabric paint on the piece of cardboard and press the stamp into the paint. Press the stamp on the fabric, wipe the surface of the stamp clean, and repeat by dipping the stamp in the paint again. If you are having trouble holding the stamp, press a pushpin into the back.

Allow for the paint to completely dry and heat-set by pressing according to the paint manufacturer's directions. Wash the stamp with warm water. If you're using multiple colors at the same time, use a paintbrush, cotton swab, or toothpick to paint individual segments. I backstitched the legs and antennae with a blended needle made of one strand of #310 black and one strand of #3799 very dark pewter gray, and I added highlights with two strands of blanc.

■ EDGING

With one strand of #327, decorate the border of the bib with randomly placed ⅛-inch (3-mm) long seed stitches. Edge the neckline with one-sided fern stitch.

■ FINISHING

When you've finished stitching, rinse the bib in three changes of cold water to remove the pen marks and any dye that may still be held in the threads. Lay flat to dry; press right side down on a terry-cloth towel.

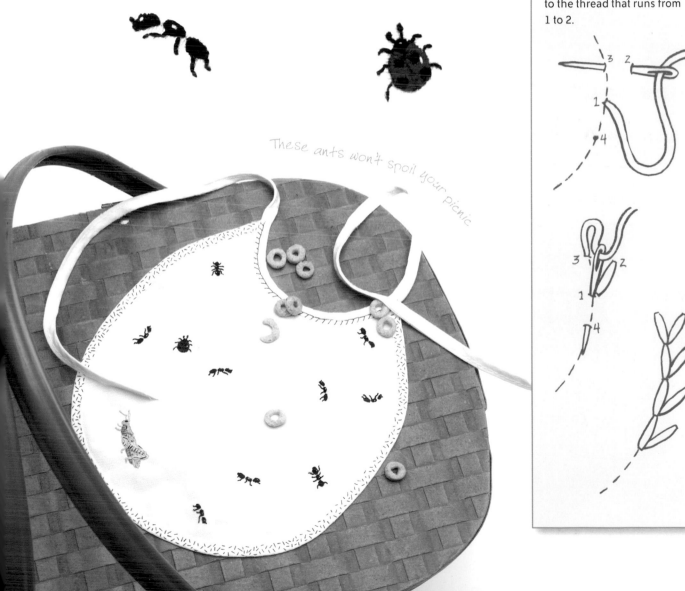

These ants won't spoil your picnic

DAY TRIPPER
BAG

Display the souvenirs from favorite places and
events on the front of this bag with the aid of iron
transfers and reverse appliqué; add a beaded strap
to dress it up. Inside, pop photographs, ticket stubs,
and other memorabilia that remind you of friends,
and you've got the makings of a fabulous gift that
won't be forgotten. The small vignettes on my
bag, which I plan to give as a birthday
gift, show the mountains I've hiked,
plays I've seen, and trips I've
taken with my friend.

■ SIZE

5½ × 4½ inches (14.0 × 11.4 cm); not including strap

■ THREADS

100% cotton 6-strand embroidery threads (I used DMC Embroidery Floss, Article 117), 8.7 yards (8 m)/skein, 1 skein each of the colors listed in the keys; beading thread (I used Nymo size B), 132 yards (120 m)/bobbin, 1 bobbin to match beads; sewing thread, deep purple

■ FABRIC

100% cotton: patterned purple, 6 × 5½ inches (15.2 × 14.0 cm), 2 pieces; 100% cotton: green, 6½ × 5½ inches (16.5 × 14.0 cm), 2 pieces; 100% cotton: deep purple, orange, and gold, 3 × 3 inches (7.6 × 7.6 cm), 2 pieces each; 100% cotton: bluish purple and green, 3 × 3 inches (7.6 × 7.6 cm), 1 piece each; Muslin fabric: 100% cotton, white, 6 × 5½ inches (15.2 × 14.0 cm), 1 piece

■ NOTIONS

Iron-on T-shirt transfer paper for ink-jet printers, 1 sheet, 11 × 8½ inches (27.9 × 21.6 cm); needles, embroidery size 9 and beading size 10; fabric-marking pen or pencil; embroidery hoop, 6 inches (15.2 cm) in diameter; beads to match the patterned fabric and your size preference, amount needed for a 6- to 8-inch (15.2- to 20.3-cm) strap
Optional: sewing machine

■ STITCHES

Running stitch, page 20
Double running stitch, page 20

■ INSTRUCTIONS

Note: Use the beading needle and beading thread only for attaching the beaded strap; use the embroidery needle for all other stitches.

Begin by scanning three of your favorite ticket stubs or photographs (or have your local copy shop create a digital version for you). Reduce or enlarge the images as necessary so that they fit as closely as possible inside one of the squares of Pattern 1. Print the images on iron-transfer paper (see sidebar on page 67 for tips); images should be no larger than 2 × 2 inches (5.1 × 5.1 cm). Remember that you will need to adjust the print or document settings on the computer to print the reverse of the image you want to portray. If you wish to print directly on the fabric, see the "Tips for Iron Transfers and Printing on Fabric" sidebar (page 67). Trim around one of the images, leaving ½ inch (1.3 cm) on all sides and iron-transfer to one of the 3-inch (7.6-cm) squares of orange, green, or gold fabric according to manufacturer's directions. Repeat iron-transferring for the other two images and 3-inch (7.6-cm) squares. Set all three pieces aside.

Using one of the transfer methods on pages 5–8, transfer the Xs of Pattern 1 to the right side of the patterned fabric. The Xs indicate the lines that will be cut for the fabric windows (see Figure 1) on the patterned fabric. The squares and rectangles you chose to reveal the ticket stubs or photographs may need to be adjusted

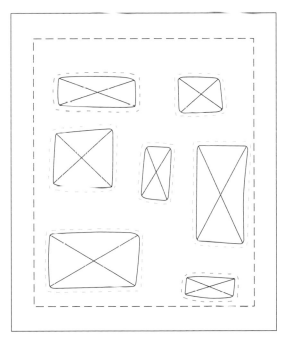

■ #3854 medium autumn gold

■ #922 light copper

■ #471 very light avocado green

Pattern 1. Front of the bag
Enlarge pattern by 198%

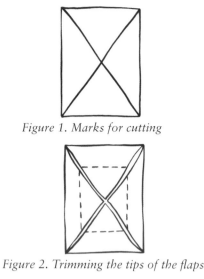

Figure 1. Marks for cutting

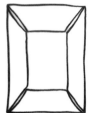

Figure 2. Trimming the tips of the flaps

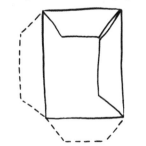

Figure 3. Trimmed flaps

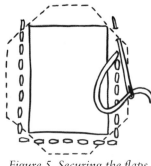

Figure 4. Folding back the flaps

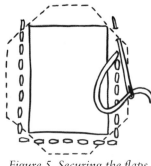

Figure 5. Securing the flaps

to fit the specific dimensions of your transferred images; adjust the size of the Xs so that the box created by the four corners of the X reflect the dimensions of your images. If the new boxes are larger than the ones on the pattern, make sure they are at least ¼ inch (6 mm) from the other boxes and edges.

Create the windows for the bag with reverse appliqué technique: Carefully trim along the Xs and trim off the tips of the fabric (see Figures 2 and 3). Fold the four flaps to the back of the fabric and press (Figure 4). Place the patterned fabric on top of the muslin and draw along the inside border of the boxes and rectangles with the marking pen or pencil and set the patterned fabric aside. Center the 3-inch (7.6-cm) squares of fabric on top of the drawn boxes; trim the fabric squares, if needed, so that they do not overlap. Baste (using large, temporary running stitches) the squares to the muslin, ⅛ inch (3 mm) outside the drawn border. Lay the patterned fabric on the muslin with the wrong side of the patterned fabric on the right side of the muslin and pin the layers together. Mount the layers of fabric in the embroidery hoop (to allow for fine adjustments during stitching, not all edges of the fabric will be secured in the hoop). Join the layers by adding running stitches around the borders, ⅛ inch (3 mm) from the folded edges (see Figure 5), referring to Pattern 1 for color placement and using two strands of thread. Remove the layers of fabric from the hoop and remove the basting stitches. *Note*: I cut an X in one of the 3-inch (7.6-cm) squares of fabric with the edges tucked back, and stitched to another 3-inch (7.6-cm) square of fabric to achieve an additional layer of reverse appliqué in one of the squares.

For the backing fabric, use the second piece of patterned fabric or cut windows in the second piece as indicated in the sidebar with the use of Pattern 2 (page 68). With the sewing thread and right sides facing, join the backing fabric to the front piece with a ½-inch (1.3–cm) seam allowance by machine stitching (or hand stitching with tightly spaced double running or backstitches) along the sides and the bottom. Trim the seam allowances to ¼ inch (6 mm); trim the corners, and turn right sides out. To achieve crisp corners, use a knitting needle or chopstick to push the corners out. Machine or hand stitch the two pieces of green lining fabric along the bottom and side seams. Turn the top edge over ½ inch (1.3 cm) and press; turn over another ½ inch (1.3 cm) and press again. Insert the green lining inside the patterned pieces, tucking the top raw edges of the patterned fabric and muslin under the fold of the green fabric. Join all layers of fabric with two strands of #922 and running stitches that are placed ⅛ inch (3 mm) above the bottom edge of the fold in the green fabric and ⅛ inch (3 mm) below the top edge of the bag. Add short, widely spaced running stitches between the rows with two strands of #3854. To add the beaded strap, thread the beading needle with beading thread, knot the end of the thread, take a stitch along the inside edge of the bag on the right, pick up the beads, and take a stitch on the inside edge on the left side. Pass back through the beads for strength and knot at the starting point.

66

TIPS FOR IRON TRANSFERS
AND PRINTING ON FABRIC

• With the number of products on the market designed for decorating and personalizing T-shirts and other everyday objects, it is easy to add images to your needlework. I have had the best results from iron-on T-shirt transfer sheets designed for use with ink-jet or bubble-jet printers. The sheets are relatively inexpensive, available at office-supply stores, and the transferred images are long-lasting and flexible. Transfer pages designed for use with copy machines often cannot withstand the heat of the machines and may melt to the machine's rollers.

• When you purchase transfer paper, keep in mind the end use. Some transfer papers are designed for use with dark fabrics. Also keep in mind the end use when you're choosing fabric—it is often best to use light-colored fabrics for your ground, especially for printing words and low-contrast detailed images. You will need to adjust the computer's document or print setup to print a reverse image when you use iron transfers.

• Be patient and follow the ironing directions on the package for transferring images. Do not pull the paper backing off before the fabric and paper have cooled.

• Be careful in using a very hot iron on other parts of your project; the transfer materials may smear and melt if touched directly with a hot iron.

• Consider printing directly on the fabric. In Chapter 1, I simply fused heavyweight nonwoven fusible web to the back of an 11- x 8½-inch (27.9- x 21.6-cm) piece of fabric and fed the paper-backed fabric through the ink-jet printer before removing the paper backing. This method is best if you are going to fuse the printed fabric to another piece of fabric after printing; if not, prepare fabric for your printer by ironing on medium heat an 11- x 8-inch (27.9- x 21.6-cm) piece of freezer paper (available at grocery stores) to an 11- x 8½-inch (27.9- x 21.6-cm) piece of fabric with the waxy side of the freezer paper facing the wrong side of the fabric. Many textile craft suppliers now carry freezer paper that is designed for this type of printing and is thicker, more adhesive and, depending on the fabric, reusable up to four times. This paper may be packaged for appliqué and a fabric-piecing technique called foundation paper piecing. You will not need to print the reverse image as you do when you use iron transfers.

• If the fabric you are printing on is going to be washed and heavily used and is not a purchased fabric-covered sheet, pretreat the fabric by soaking it in Bubble Jet Set 2000, a product made specifically for printing on cotton and silk fabric with an ink-jet or bubble-jet printer; it's available from many textile craft suppliers. Back the treated fabric with heavyweight nonwoven fusible web or freezer paper. Bubble Jet Set Rinse is a mild detergent for laundering dyed and printed fabrics. You must wear gloves and maintain proper ventilation when you use these products.

• If you wish to print on white fabric but don't want to back the fabric yourself with fusible web or freezer paper, you may purchase fabric-covered sheets of paper for ink-jet and bubble-jet printers. When printing is complete you can simply tear off the paper backing and use the fabric for any sewing project. Although this step keeps you from having to back the fabric yourself, your palette is limited to white. These sheets are available in cotton and silk from craft, quilt, and some office supply stores.

QUILTING BASICS: PIECING AND QUILT TYING

Patchwork piecing, the technique used to create the background fabric for the optional reverse appliquéd back of the bag, is basic to making quilt tops. If you learn this technique, not only will you be able to piece and design fabrics for things like bags and pillows (which you can then embellish with embroidery), you will have the ability to make a quilt top of any size. Although best sewn with a sewing machine, pieces may also be joined with tightly spaced double running or backstitches. Here, you will learn how to construct the background fabric for the reverse appliquéd back of the Day Tripper's bag, how to apply this technique on a larger scale to make a quilt top, and the basics of tying and finishing a quilt.

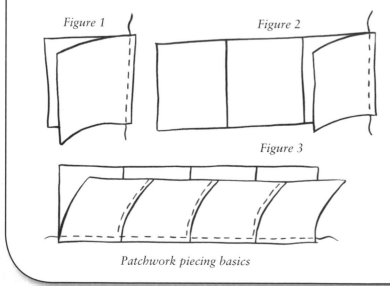

Figure 1

Figure 2

Figure 3

Patchwork piecing basics

Piecing Basics

A few simple steps make piecing quick and easy. Use a ¼-inch (6-mm) seam allowance for each seam. Referring to Figure 1, join two squares of fabric along the right side with right sides facing. Referring to Figure 2, join another square to the right side of the previously joined square with right sides facing; repeat to make a strip. Press all seam allowances to one side and set aside the strip of fabric. Repeat the steps shown in Figures 1 and 2 to make another strip of joined squares; press the seam allowances in the opposite direction you pressed the seam allowances in the first strip. Referring to Figure 3, join the strips: To make sure that the seams line up, pin strips together before sewing the seam (puckering will occur if you force the previously sewn seams of the strips to line up; the pins are only used to make slight adjustments). Sew the strips together and press the seam allowances to one side.

Making the Back of the Day Tripper's Bag

To create the base fabric for the back of the bag with the patchwork piecing technique, you will need twenty 1⅞-inch (4.8-cm) squares of contrasting fabric, sewing thread the same color value as a majority of the fabric squares, a sewing machine (preferable), and pins. Use a sewing machine or tightly spaced double running or backstitches and the patchwork piecing technique to join five of the squares, end to end, with a ¼-inch (6-mm) seam allowance, to make a strip that is five squares long. Press the seam allowances to one side. Make three more strips that are each five squares long. Pin and join the strips along the longest sides with a ¼-inch (6-mm) seam allowance and press the seam allowances to one side. The result is a pieced fabric that is four by five squares. Using Pattern 2 as a guide, cut Xs to create windows in the second piece of 6- × 5 ½-inch (15.2- × 14.0-cm) patterned fabric called for in this chapter. Trim and tuck back the flaps, and then sew down the flaps of the Xs with running stitches as directed for the front of the bag (see page 66).

Making a Patchwork Quilt Top

Create your own pieced quilt with the patchwork piecing technique. The size of the quilt and individual squares will determine how many squares make up a strip. To make a twin size quilt, make the pieced squares equal 86 × 68 inches

(218.4 × 172.7 cm); for a double/queen size, make the pieced squares equal 86 × 86 inches (218.4 × 218.4 cm); for a king size quilt, make the pieced squares equal 86 × 101 inches (218.4 × 256.5 cm). Press the seams to one side.

Constructing and Finishing a Tied Quilt

To finish the quilt with the tying technique (joining the pieced top fabric with backing fabric and batting with small ties), you will need: A piece of high-quality backing fabric the same size and fiber content as the pieced quilt top (depending on the size of your quilt, you may need to do some piecing), safety pins, pieced-quilt top, quilt batting (sold in rolls or large sheets), 1-inch (2.5-cm) wide double-fold bias tape

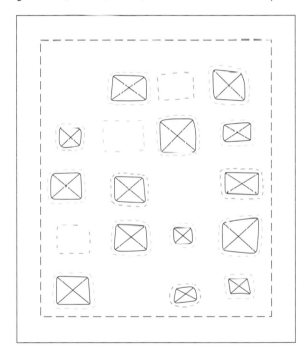

#3854 medium autumn gold

#922 light copper

#471 very light avocado green

Pattern 2. Back of the bag. Enlarge pattern by 198%

binding, and a size 16 chenille needle (all amounts needed are determined by the size of your quilt).

Spread the backing fabric out on the floor, wrong side up, and cover with a sheet of quilt batting; follow manufacturer's directions if you need to join strips of batting for a large quilt (some brands suggest using a machine zigzag stitch to join the edges of the batting). With right sides facing up, spread the pieced quilt top over the batting and backing fabric, sandwiching the batting. Smooth the layers with your hands and use safety pins to temporarily join the layers. Starting from the center, pins should be placed no more than 6 inches (15.2 cm) apart. If you have trouble joining the layers and closing regular safety pins, use curved pins designed specifically for quilting. After all the pins are dispersed across the fabrics, you may pick up the layers and work on your lap, on the floor, or you may mount the layers of fabric in a quilting frame or embroidery hoop that is 14 inches (35.6 cm) in diameter or larger. To begin tying, thread the chenille needle with the yarn and, from the right side, take a stitch through all the layers, remove the needle, and double knot and trim the ends of the yarn. Repeat across the entire quilt, with the ties no more than 4 inches (10.2 cm) from each other. Once all the ties have been placed, spread out the layers again on the floor and trim around the quilt to make all layers the same size.

To edge with bias binding, unfold the binding and lay it on top of the quilt with right sides facing. Align one long edge of the binding with the outside edge of the quilt, in the middle of one of the sides, and pin the body of the binding to all layers of fabric. Join the binding to the quilt, sewing along the fold in the binding closest to the outside edges of the fabric. Carefully turn and notch the binding when you sew around corners: With scissors, clip small ¼-inch (6-mm) notches along the outside edge of the binding and around the corners of the fabrics and binding. If you run out of binding, you will need to join the short ends of the binding with another piece. As you approach the starting point, trim the end of the binding so that it extends over the starting point by 1½ inches (3.8 cm). Fold back the raw end of the binding ½ inch (1.3 cm) before you cover the starting point.

Fold the bias tape lengthwise along the manufacturer's creases to the back, covering the raw edges of the fabrics and enclosing the batting. To secure the binding, slip-stitch it to the back of the quilt along the manufacturer's outside fold.

CAPTURED BUTTERFLY
PICTURE FRAME

Stumpwork enlivens needlework by adding dimension. In this project, the wings of a butterfly are suspended above the frame's embroidered background with wire; to omit the wire, you can combine the patterns and stitch the butterfly directly on the background fabric.

■ SIZE	■ THREADS	■ FABRIC	■ NOTIONS	■ STITCHES
7 × 5 inches (17.8 × 12.7 cm); not including frame	100% silk 6-strand embroidery threads (I used YLI), 5.5 yards (5 m)/pack, 1 pack each of the colors listed in the keys	100% cotton: aqua blue, 11 × 11 inches (27.9 × 27.9 cm), 1 piece; 100% cotton: purple, 6 × 6 inch (15.2 × 15.2 cm), 2 pieces; Fleece: white, 9 × 7 inches (22.9 × 17.8 cm), 1 piece	Medium-weight nonwoven fusible interfacing, 11 × 11 inches (27.9 × 27.9 cm), 1 piece; stumpwork wire, cloth-covered, 32-gauge wire, 8 inches (20.3 cm) long, 2 pieces; needles, chenille size 18 and embroidery size 10; embroidery hoops, 5 inches (12.7 cm), 10 inches (25.4 cm) in diameter; mat board, 7 × 5 inches (17.8 × 12.7 cm) with a 2¾- × 1¾-inch (7.0- × 4.5-cm) opening; X-acto knife; wire cutters; acid-free craft glue	Buttonhole stitch, below Colonial knots, page 35 Couching, page 21 Long-and-short satin stitch, page 20 Satin over double running stitch, page 30 Stem stitch, page 21

■ INSTRUCTIONS

Note: Unless otherwise noted, use one strand of silk and the embroidery needle for all stitches. Refer to the patterns for color placement.

■ WINGS

Using one of the transfer methods on pages 5–8, transfer wing pattern (Pattern 1, page 72) to the center of one of the purple pieces of fabric. Mount the fabric in the 5-inch (12.7-cm) hoop. Using the outline of the wing pattern as a guide, bend the wire to match the shape of the wing. Bend the tails of the wires according to the pattern so they are parallel to each other and at right angles to the outline of the wing (do not couch the wire after the right angle bends). Use #819 to couch down the wire every ⅛ inch (3 mm) along the outline of the wing. Outline the eyespots with double running stitch; fill and cover the outlines with vertical satin stitches. Use long-and-short satin stitch to fill the background and accent lines of the wing; when you're working close to the outer edge, angle the stitches under the wire. Completely cover the wire with buttonhole stitches, starting and stopping at the right-angle bends in the wire. Remove the fabric from the hoop. Center and transfer the other wing (Pattern 2, page 72) to the second piece of purple fabric, mount in the hoop, repeat wire bending and stitching instructions as for the first wing, and remove the fabric from the hoop.

Leaving about a ¼ inch (6 mm) of fabric between the uncovered wires to create a flap, carefully trim the fabric around the buttonhole stitches with embroidery scissors. To straighten stitches, lightly brush the edge of the stitches with your finger and trim the loosened fabric threads. Fold the flap under the wing so that the long-and-short stitches are at the edge of the fabric; tack the flap to the back with a few satin stitches. Repeat trimming and stitching for the other wing and set both pieces aside.

■ BACKGROUND

Fuse the interfacing to the back of the blue fabric according to manufacturer's directions and use one of the transfer methods on pages 5–8 to transfer the background pattern

BUTTONHOLE STITCH

This stitch is a tightly worked blanket stitch (page 89). Working the stitches from left to right, bring the needle up at 1 and insert at 2. (For stumpwork, the thread between these two points covers the wire.) Bring the needle up at 3 and over the working thread. To achieve an even edge, keep the needle low to the fabric and pull the needle toward you while tightening the loop; make each new stitch as close to the previous one as possible.

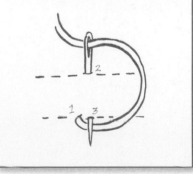

Pattern 1   Pattern 2

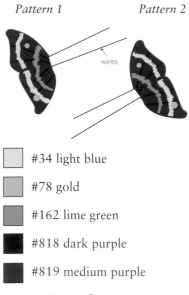

wires

☐ #34 light blue

☐ #78 gold

☐ #162 lime green

■ #818 dark purple

■ #819 medium purple

Butterfly wings
Enlarge patterns by 185%

Pattern 3. Background pattern
Enlarge pattern by 200%

(Pattern 3), excluding the dashed lines in the center of the fabric. Mount the fabric in the 10-inch (25.4-cm) embroidery hoop and refer to the pattern for color placement. Stem stitch the branches and antennae with two strands of silk thread and the lime green highlights with one strand (use one strand of each color for the blended needles). Stitch the dark purple dots of the pattern with two strands and colonial knots. Use a single strand of thread to outline the body and tail with double running stitches; fill and cover the outlines with satin stitches, using vertical satin stitches for the body of the butterfly and horizontal satin stitches for the tail and its three light blue highlights.

■ ATTACHING THE WINGS

Make sure that the blue fabric is taut in the embroidery hoop. Referring to the red dots of the pattern for placement, punch holes in the fabric with the chenille needle on either side of the butterfly body. Pull the wires of the left wing through the two holes on the left side of the body. Wrap your hand around the hoop and hold the wings in place. Looking at the right side of the fabric, make sure the long-and-short satin stitches on the base of the wing are flush against the background fabric; if they are not, the wires need to be pulled a little tighter from the back. Bend the wires toward the center of the wing at the point at which the wires emerge from the front; wires will be flush with the back of the fabric. Tack the wires with two strands of #818 and satin stitch under the body of the butterfly. Attach the right wing by bringing the wires through the two holes on the right side of the body, repeat pulling and wire bending, and tack the wires to the back of the fabric. Use caution if you have to retwist the wire more than once; the wire may break. Wrap the four wires with thread to create a small bundle where they meet under the body. Trim the uncovered wire tails. If the fabric at the base of the wings is showing, add a few more vertical satin stitches to the center of the butterfly's body with the embroidery needle. Gently bend the wings on the front so that the tips are suspended about 1/8 inch (3mm) above the ground fabric. Remove the fabric from the hoop and set aside.

■ ASSEMBLING THE FRAME

Lightly coat the right side of the mat board with glue, let dry for about two minutes; center and place right side down on the fleece. Allow the layers to dry on a flat surface under the weight of a book. When the glue is completely dry, lay the frame right side down on a cutting mat or piece of cardboard and use the X-acto knife to cut the fleece out of the opening in the mat. Trim the fleece around the mat and set aside.

☐ #34 light blue

■ #162 lime green

■ #818 dark purple

■ #818 dark purple and #819 medium purple blended needle

Trim the background fabric within 1 inch (2.5 cm) of the outside dashed line and gently lay right side down on a hard surface covered with a terry-cloth towel. Lightly coat the outer ½-inch (1.3-cm) of the back of the mat with glue and center the mat with the fleece side down on the wrong side of the background fabric. First pull the corners of the background fabric, then the sides, onto the glued mat with tight and even tension. Let dry for a minimum of five minutes. With the fabric right side down on a cutting mat positioned on the edge of a table and the butterfly hanging off the edge, draw an X in the center that extends from one corner of the mat's opening to another. Starting and stopping ⅛ inch (3mm) from the tips of the drawn X, cut along the X with the X-acto knife; trim ¼ inch (6 mm) off the points. Working on the wrong side of the fabric, lightly coat with glue the top ¼ inch (6 mm) of the trimmed flaps, tightly pull the flaps to the back, and glue to the back of the mat. Mount the mat in your favorite picture frame.

WORKING WITH SILK AND WIRE

Working with silk and wire is fun and results in beautiful objects; however, these materials may intimidate those new to embroidery. Here are some tips:

• In working with silk, make sure your hands are clean and moisturized; dry hands can snag the silk and frustrate the stitcher.

• It is helpful to lightly pull the silk thread through nontoxic, acid-free thread conditioner, like Thread Heaven, when you're working with multiple strands. Using thread conditioner will slightly dull the silk but it may be a necessary step when a stitcher is handling silk for the first time.

• If you are one of the many stitchers who wets your strands to thread the eye of the needle, remember that wet silk is difficult to pull through fabric. Silk is naturally weaker when it's wet.

• When you're working large areas with satin stitch and single or multiple threads, you may use a laying tool to keep the stitches uniform and in position.

• Remember that some people spend a lifetime studying silk embroidery techniques; don't expect your stitches to be perfect the first time.

• There are various types of wire on the market that are suitable for stumpwork. If you find it difficult to find cloth-covered stumpwork wire, consider using white thread- or paper-covered 32-gauge wire. Color the wire covering with a permanent marker. If your buttonhole stitches are tightly worked you can use plain, uncovered 22 gauge wire.

• Covered wire is sometimes difficult to pull through fabric. If necessary, increase the size of the holes in the ground fabric or lightly coat the ends of the wire with glue—you may also wrap them with a small piece of tape—to prevent the ground fabric from pushing back the material that covers the wire.

• Consider investing in wire-working tools. Use needle-nose pliers for stumpwork projects that require frequent bends in the wire and high-quality wire cutters for crisp and consistent cuts.

• If you are doing stumpwork and working with several pieces of wire, you may build bulk on the back of the fabric. To hide a small lump created by the wires, back the embroidery with fleece, as explained on page 72. To hide a large lump, cut a hole in the fleece below the wires.

GIFT TAGS, CARDS, AND NOTEBOOKS

If you enjoy breaking the rules and making design decisions on the fly, you'll love this project: Machine embroidery is a breeze when you have the freedom to stitch in any direction. Created on a dissolvable surface, these hip, free-form shapes are a uniquely stitched web of threads; the thickness of your stitches can make them dense or airy. In doing this project, you'll become familiar with your machine's tension, stitch settings, and feed dogs.

S P E C I F I C A T I O N S

■ SIZE

Finished sizes of designs
Gift tag: 2 × ¾ inches
(5.1 × 1.9 cm)
Block: 2¾ × 2¾ inches
(7.0 ×7.0 cm)
House: 2½ × 2½ inches
(6.4 × 6.4 cm)
Martini glass:
2¾ × 2 inches
(7.0 × 5.1 cm)

■ THREADS

Sewing thread,
100% cot-
ton, 1 spool
each of warm
purple, blue
purple, dark
sage green, lime
green, red, deep
red, magenta,
teal, and white

■ NOTIONS

Water soluble stabilizer (I used Super Solvy
Heavier Water Soluble Stabilizer by Sulky),
5 × 5 inches (12.7 × 12.7 cm), 8 pieces;
embroidery hoop (preferably one with an
inner wire ring and outer plastic ring),
5 inches (12.7 cm) in diameter; acid-free
craft glue; tags, cards, notebook, in the
sizes of your choice; permanent marker;
sewing machine

■ STITCH

Free-form zigzag
stitch

■ INSTRUCTIONS

Mount two layers of water soluble stabilizer in an embroidery hoop suitable for machine embroidery with the inner hoop on top of the fabric (page 8). With a permanent marker and the stabilizer centered and resting on top of the pattern, trace around the outlines of the motif.

To prepare the machine, drop the feed dogs (the machine's mechanism on the faceplate that moves fabric under the foot) and release the presser foot (usually a dial or knob on the front of the machine); see the sewing machine illustration on page 109. On some machines, a plate covers the feed dogs. Set the stitch width on the machine just short of the widest setting (I set mine to 4) to create zigzags; you control the stitch length by moving the hoop under the presser foot.

Fill the shapes with the colors indicated on page 76 by moving the hoop back and forth across the area to be filled, in all directions and at a consistent speed. Once you are comfortable with free-form machine embroidery, experiment with changing the stitch width and the speed at which you move the hoop. For a very slight shift in color, change the bobbin thread. Changing the top thread results in an overall shift in color. You can achieve a dramatic shift in color by changing both the top and bottom thread. For these beginner projects, the bobbins are changed at random for an underlying hint of color. See the "Understanding and Using your Sewing Machine's Tension" sidebar on page 77 for tips on manipulating tension for design. If you would like to experiment with threads other than cotton, wind thick or metallic threads in the bobbin to prevent them from traveling through the needle; remember that you will now be viewing the back of the design as you stitch. If this is your first experience with free-form machine embroidery, start with the notebook's color blocks.

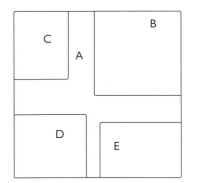

Blocks
Enlarge pattern by 158%

■ BLOCKS

First fill four bobbins with the red, warm purple, lime green, and teal sewing thread; Switch them at random to become familiar with the effects created by the underlying color. Work the middle crosslike shape (A) with light layers of lime green and teal top threads and cover with blue purple; extend these borders out to the edges of the corner blocks so the stitches overlap. Work the top right corner (B) with thin base layers of red and warm purple top thread and cover with a layer of dark sage green top thread. Work the top left corner (C) with a base layer of red top thread and cover with a layer of warm purple. Work the bottom left corner (D) with a base layer of lime green top thread and cover with a layer of teal. Work the bottom right corner (E) with a base layer of dark sage green top thread and cover with a layer of red.

■ HOUSE

Switch bobbin threads among red, deep red, and purple while you stitch. With purple in the top thread, quickly stitch the entire house—do not build stitches in a specific area. Cover the top of the house and door (A) with purple top thread; fill the rest of the house (B) by switching between the shades of red. Work the roof (C) with thick stitches and red thread—start at the top of the house and slowly move the hoop so that the stitches are right next to each other and resemble satin stitch (page 20). Cover the other side of the roof with satin stitches in the same manner. Lightly stitch over the top and right side of the house with blue-purple thread.

■ GIFT TAG AND MARTINI GLASS

Work the martini glass and gift tag designs with a base layer of teal top thread (I worked both shapes with lime green, deep purple, and a little bit of white bobbin thread). Referring to the patterns for color placement, work A with blue purple, B with warm purple, C with lime green, D with teal, and E with magenta.

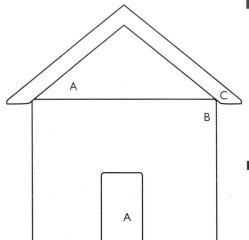

House

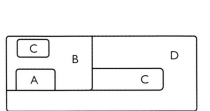

Gift tag

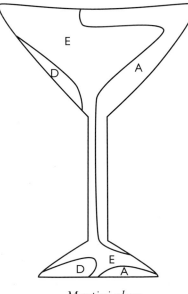

Martini glass

■ FINISHING

Once the entire design area is covered with stitches, check the thickness. For a sturdy object, build stitches so they are ⅛ inch (3 mm) thick. When you are satisfied with the shape, trim the stabilizer to within ⅛ inch (3 mm) of the motif. For lacey objects, stitch just until the point where all stitches overlap; you should be able to see through some of the stabilizer. Fill a bowl with warm water and allow the stitching to soak for two minutes; blot dry on a towel. If the stitching is too stiff when it's dry, soak until the desired amount of stabilizer is dissolved. Heavily stitched pieces will need to be soaked longer than open, lacey stitches. The integrity of lacey designs may be compromised if too much of the stabilizer is dissolved.

To finish the house-warming card, cocktail party invitation, or gift tag, lightly coat the wrong side of the design with acid-free glue. Adhere the pieces to store-bought or handmade blank cards and allow to dry under the weight of a book. To create the notebook, simply insert the piece into the notebook's window and, if necessary, tape or glue in place.

Such clever gift tags!

UNDERSTANDING AND USING YOUR SEWING MACHINE'S TENSION

Knowing how to control a machine's tension is essential to basic sewing, the life of the machine, and the appearance of free-form embroidered pieces.

When the tension is balanced, the top thread and bobbin thread should meet in the center of the fabric. The bobbin thread should not be visible on the right side of the fabric just as the top thread should not be visible on the wrong side of the fabric (Figure 1).

When the bobbin thread is seen on the right side of the fabric, either the tension of the top thread is too tight or the bobbin thread is too loose (Figure 2).

When the top thread is seen on the wrong side of the fabric, either the tension of the top thread is too loose or the bobbin thread is too tight (Figure 3).

To adjust the tension of the top thread, turn the dial on the top of most machines. To adjust the tension of the bobbin thread, make small adjustments to the screw on the bobbin case. Loosen the tension by turning to the left; tighten the tension by turning to the right.

Subtle changes to a design may be achieved by intentionally setting a machine's tension off balance. Instead of changing the color of the thread when you're shading or highlighting a design, simply adjust the tension to hide or reveal the top and bobbin threads.

Figure 1. Balanced tension

Figure 2. Tight top thread or loose bobbin thread

Figure 3. Tight bobbin thread or loose top thread

GUITAR PICK CASE

A hand-embroidered pouch is a great way to store guitar picks.
This gift is fun to make, and your special guitarist will sing
your praises for such a hip present. The outside of the
pick case is decorated with fun polka dots and
music composition basics: whole,
half, and quarter notes.

The pick case is as portable as this backpacker guitar

■ SIZE	■ THREADS	■ FABRIC	■ NOTIONS	■ STITCHES
2¼ × 1¼ inches (5.7 × 3.2 cm)	100% cotton 6-strand embroidery threads (I used DMC Embroidery Floss, Article 117), 8.7 yards (8 m)/skein, 1 skein each of the colors listed in the keys	100% cotton: orange, 7 × 7 inches (17.8 × 17.8 cm), 2 pieces; 100% cotton: orange, 3 × 3 inches (7.6 × 7.6 cm), 2 pieces	Lightweight nonwoven fusible interfacing, 3 × 3 inches (7.6 × 7.6 cm), 2 pieces; needles, embroidery sizes 10 and 8; embroidery hoop, 6 inches (15.2 cm) in diameter; liquid seam sealant (Fray Check)	Bound satin stitch, page 81 Couching, page 21 Double running stitch, page 20 Overcast stitch, page 21 Running stitch, page 20 Satin over double running stitch, page 30

■ INSTRUCTIONS

Note: Use the size 10 needle to work with one strand; use the size 8 needle for all other stitches. Refer to the patterns for color placement.

Using one of the transfer methods on pages 5–8, transfer Pattern 1 to the center of one of the 7-inch (17.8-cm) squares of fabric. Mount the fabric in the hoop. Outline all the notes and polka dots with double running stitches and two strands of thread. Fill the solid shapes with satin stitch and two strands of thread, covering the double running stitches. Use overcast stitch for the vertical lines of the notes.

To fill the background, couch down four strands of #3051 with one strand of #3768; work around the perimeter of the polka dots and notes. Once you have circled one motif three to four times, bring the couched thread to the back of the fabric and begin working around the perimeter of another motif. When you've filled around all the notes and polka dots, use couching to fill in the remainder of the background by extending some of the lines around the notes. If you reach the edge of the design, simply take the couched thread to the back of the fabric and bring it up next to the previous row to start the next concentric circle. Remove the fabric from the hoop.

Transfer Pattern 2 (page 81) to the center of the second 7-inch (17.8-cm) square and mount the square in the hoop. Fill the motifs, background, and running-stitch border as directed above but use one strand of #3051 to couch down four strands of #3768 when you fill the background. Remove the fabric from the hoop.

Using one of the 3-inch (7.6-cm) pieces of fusible web and referring to the manufacturer's directions, fuse one of the 3-inch (7.6-cm) orange squares to the center of the wrong side of the embroidered pieces with the embroidery right side down on a terry-cloth towel. Mount the layers of fabric in the hoop and

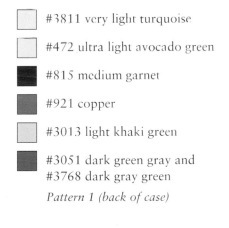

	#3811 very light turquoise
	#472 ultra light avocado green
	#815 medium garnet
	#921 copper
	#3013 light khaki green
	#3051 dark green gray and #3768 dark gray green

Pattern 1 (back of case)

MANAGING COUCHED THREADS

When you're working tight areas with couched and couching threads, it is easy to cross and tangle the threads. To avoid such snarls, use the following tips for keeping couched threads out of the couching thread's stitching path:

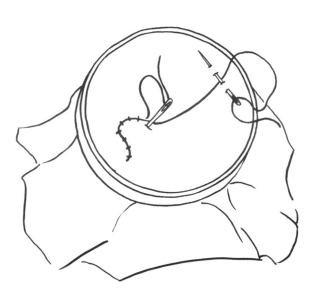

Figure 1. Managing the couched thread

• Keep couched threads short. Couched threads longer than 16 inches (40.6 cm) are hard to keep separated from the finer couching thread.

• Consider storing the long thread to be couched off the edge of the hoop (Figure 1). Pull the couched thread away from the design area and temporarily tack it down with the second needle: With the needle that holds the couched thread, pick up 1/8 inch (3 mm) of fabric near the outside border of the hoop, tuck the couched thread under the needle, and then pick up another 1/8 inch (3 mm) of fabric; leave the needle in the fabric. Pull the couched thread taut. Temporarily storing a needle in this way is often referred to as "parking the needle."

• When you're working straight lines, consider inserting the couched thread into the fabric at the end of the design line to be covered and bringing the needle up at the beginning of the next area to be stitched (as opposed to holding the couched thread to the fabric with your hand). The thread naturally creates a straight line between the beginning and end points, stays taut during couching, and keeps you from having to hold the couched thread.

• If you are covering large areas that don't require the couched thread to be inserted into the fabric very often, consider removing the needle that holds the couched thread. It may require more time to manage the second needle than it takes to rethread the needle.

• Wrap the end of the couched thread around a pencil or piece of scrap fabric and unroll as needed. If you use a pencil, take the needle off the thread before wrapping. If you use a scrap of fabric, insert the needle into the scrap and wrap the thread around the fabric and needle; doing so also keeps the needle of the couched thread tucked away (you often overlook the second needle until you accidentally prick yourself).

stitch a double-running-stitch border around the design, at the base of the couched stitches, with two strands of #815. Remove the fabrics from the hoop. Trim the fabric within ⅛ inch (3 mm) of the double running stitches and lightly cover the raw edge with liquid seam sealant. Repeat the fusing and double running stitches on the second embroidered piece, using the remaining 3-inch (7.6-cm) squares of orange fabric and fusible web.

With bound satin stitch and two strands of #815, cover the edges of both pieces of fused and trimmed fabric as indicated in purple on the patterns.

With wrong sides facing, stack the front and back embroidered pieces with the bottom round edges aligned and the small piece on top. Align and baste the two pieces together: Thread the embroidery needle with one strand of #815 and insert through the front and back pieces on the inside of the running stitches; do not pull the thread tight; tie the two ends of the thread together and trim the ends. Repeat basting twice along the sides and end before the previously bound edges. Starting at the bottom of the pick case, use two strands of #815 to join the top piece to the bottom piece with bound satin stitch and work stitches to the left until you reach the previously bound edges. To cover the remaining raw edge, start the bound satin stitches on the bottom of the pick case and work to the right. If it becomes difficult to pull the needle through the fabric, use a rubber needle-pulling disk or needle gripping tube; see page 9. Use two strands of #3013 to couch down six strands of #3768 along the base of the satin stitches on the top inside curve, making sure to hide the knots and thread tails inside the pick case (see "Hiding Knots and Thread Tails" sidebar, page 27). Insert the guitar picks and close by tucking the top flap into the body of the case, over the picks.

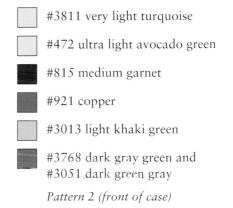

	#3811 very light turquoise
	#472 ultra light avocado green
	#815 medium garnet
	#921 copper
	#3013 light khaki green
	#3768 dark gray green and #3051 dark green gray

Pattern 2 (front of case)

Helps keep track of picks . . .

see page 9.

BOUND SATIN STITCH

Hide the thread knot between the two layers of fabric to be joined, close to the raw edges, and bring the needle out on the back. Wrap the thread around the raw edges of the two pieces of fabric by inserting the needle on top of the fabric ⅛ inch (3 mm) from the raw edges. Repeat, keeping stitches close to each other to completely cover the edges of the fabric. If you're working on medium- or lightweight fabrics, first add a row of running stitches ¹⁄₁₆ inch (1.5 mm) from the raw edges; cover the running stitches as you work the bound satin stitch.

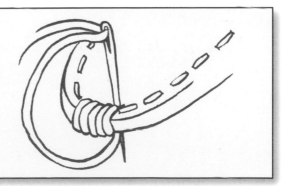

Here's a way to hang on to an unforgettable trip

■ SIZE	■ THREADS	■ FABRIC	■ NOTIONS	■ STITCHES
Finished design: 2½ × 2½ inches (6.4 × 6.4 cm)	100% cotton 6-strand embroidery threads, (I used DMC Embroidery Floss, Article 117), 8.7 yards (8 m)/skein, 1 skein each of #815 medium garnet, #920 medium copper, #924 very dark gray green, and #3371 black brown (or use the colors of your choice)	100% cotton: sage green, 7 × 7 inches (17.8 × 17.8 cm), 1 piece	Needle, embroidery size 9; photo album, in the color of your choice (I used a Kolo photograph album, Newbury, chocolate, 8½ × 10 inch [21.6 × 25.4 cm], with a 2½ inch [6.4 cm] square window); embroidery hoop, 6 inches (15.2 cm) in diameter; photocopy of a map; permanent marker, fine point, black; fabric-marking pen or pencil	Backstitch, page 20 Colonial knots, page 35 Coral stitch, page 84 Couching, page 21 Running stitch, page 20 Satin stitch, page 20

MAP
YOUR FAVORITE ESCAPE

Road trip! Stitch a map of your favorite hike, drive, or bike trip to identify the photographs in your album. Or stitch your fantasy trip—the one you'll take someday, some way—even if only in your imagination. Outline roads, boundaries, waterways, trails, and favorite stops that are meaningful to you and your friends. Try your hand at designing when you choose, resize, and draw your own map—if you dream of visiting Mt. Evans Wilderness in Colorado, use the pattern provided.

CORAL STITCH

Work the stitch from right to left by bringing the needle up at the beginning of the line at 1. Holding the thread on the line to be covered, insert the needle perpendicular to the line at 2, pick up a few threads of the fabric, and pull the needle through the loop over the working thread. Pull the thread taut to create the knot and repeat.

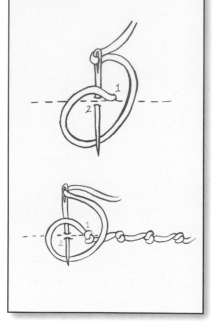

■ INSTRUCTIONS

Draw or photocopy the map of your journey and draw a square around the areas you want your embroidery to include. Working on the photocopy with the permanent marker, draw over the paths you wish to highlight in your embroidery and outline the important reference points like roads, waterways, and county/state boundaries. Reduce or enlarge the drawing or photocopy so that the drawn square is 2½ inches (6.4 cm) square.

Draw a 2½-inch (6.4-cm) square in the center of the fabric with the fabric-marking pen or pencil. Using one of the transfer methods on pages 5–8 and referring to the Mt. Evans map for general placement, transfer your map's mileage bar (or only a portion depending on the amount of space) to the bottom right-hand corner. Draw a box around the mileage bar, map's name, and compass to create the legend.

Using one of the transfer methods on pages 5–8, transfer the lines you outlined on the map inside the 2½-inch (6.4 cm) square you drew on the fabric. Do not let the lines overlap the legend area. Mount the fabric in the embroidery hoop and stitch the outlines; feel free to experiment with different stitches. Unless otherwise indicated, all the stitches on my map were worked with the embroidery needle and two strands of thread.

Stitch the roads with #3371 in backstitch, the trails with #920 in running stitch, and the mountains (indicated by triangles made of three backstitches) in #815. To stitch the lakes, couch down two strands of #924 with one strand of thread the same color in a spiral starting from the center of the lake. Stitch the streams and rivers by couching down two strands of #924 with one strand of thread in the same color. Outline the mileage bar by couching down two strands of #924 with one strand of thread in the same color, and by satin-stitching the center bar and the border of the map's legend with #815 in coral knot stitch. Couch down the outlines of the compass with one strand of thread (I used #920); add one colonial knot to the center. Remove the fabric from the hoop and trim as needed to fit the window of your photo album; I trimmed mine to 3¼ inches (8.3 cm) square.

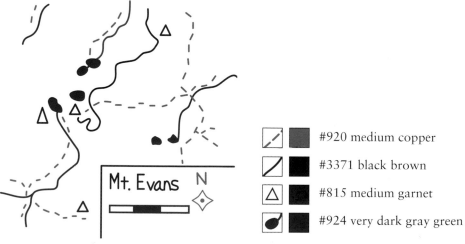

/	■	#920 medium copper
/	■	#3371 black brown
△	■	#815 medium garnet
◗	■	#924 very dark gray green

DESIGNING AN EMBROIDERED MAP

There are endless possibilities when it comes to drawing and designing maps. No matter what scale you choose to work with, here are a few basic design tips:

• Keep your map simple. Don't include too many points of interest or the design will become cluttered and confusing. Choose only the areas that are important to you. I chose lakes, rivers, trails, roads, and mountain peaks for my map to indicate a mountain park. If you choose to feature an entire state or country, choose only the points necessary to reference the areas and places of interest. For example, if you're stitching the United States to commemorate a drive across the country, consider stitching only the roads you traveled, your favorite stopping points, and a few state boundaries.

• Limit your palette to four or five colors of the same value (the relative lightness or darkness of a color); using too many colors will make the map difficult to read. Choosing colors of the same value will guarantee that the colors will blend together.

• Avoid using light colors that can show dust and wear over time. As a photo album cover, the embroidery needs to withstand years of use.

• Avoid using stitches with long and unstable thread floats (see page 30 for tips on choosing durable stitches).

• To reduce the time it takes to make the embroidered map, consider stitching on an actual map. Fuse a piece of medium-weight interfacing to the back of a paper map according to the manufacturer's directions and stitch the areas of interest with contrasting threads. When you're stitching on paper, remember to gently pull the needle through the paper and plan your stitches carefully—holes left by misplaced stitches cannot be corrected. You will not need to mount the paper in an embroidery hoop to stitch the map. Keep in mind that stitching on paper will eventually dull your needle.

■ **SIZE**

24 × 36 inches
(61.0 × 91.4 cm)

■ **THREADS**

100% cotton
6-strand embroi-
dery threads
(I used DMC
Embroidery Floss,
Article 117),
8.7 yards (8 m)/
skein, 1 skein each
of the colors listed
in the keys

■ **FABRIC**

Tea towels,
100% cot-
ton, 2 (see
the sidebar
on page 90
to make
your own)

■ **NOTIONS**

Needles,
embroidery
sizes 7 and 9;
embroidery
hoop, 6 inches
(15.2 cm) in
diameter

■ **STITCHES**

Backstitch, page 20
Chain stitch, page 21
Colonial knots, page 35
Long-and-short blanket stitch,
page 89
Seed stitch, page 20
Split stitch, page 21
Whipped backstitch, page 89

FOR
THE
HOME

CONVERSION KITCHEN
TOWELS

Keep cooking measurement conversions at your fingertips
with these vibrant, personalized tea towels. They make
charming and memorable housewarming gifts, but you
may want to make some for yourself so you won't
have to thumb through your cookbooks. Everyone
loves the bold colors and blanket-stitched edging
that evoke memories of 1950s vintage towels.

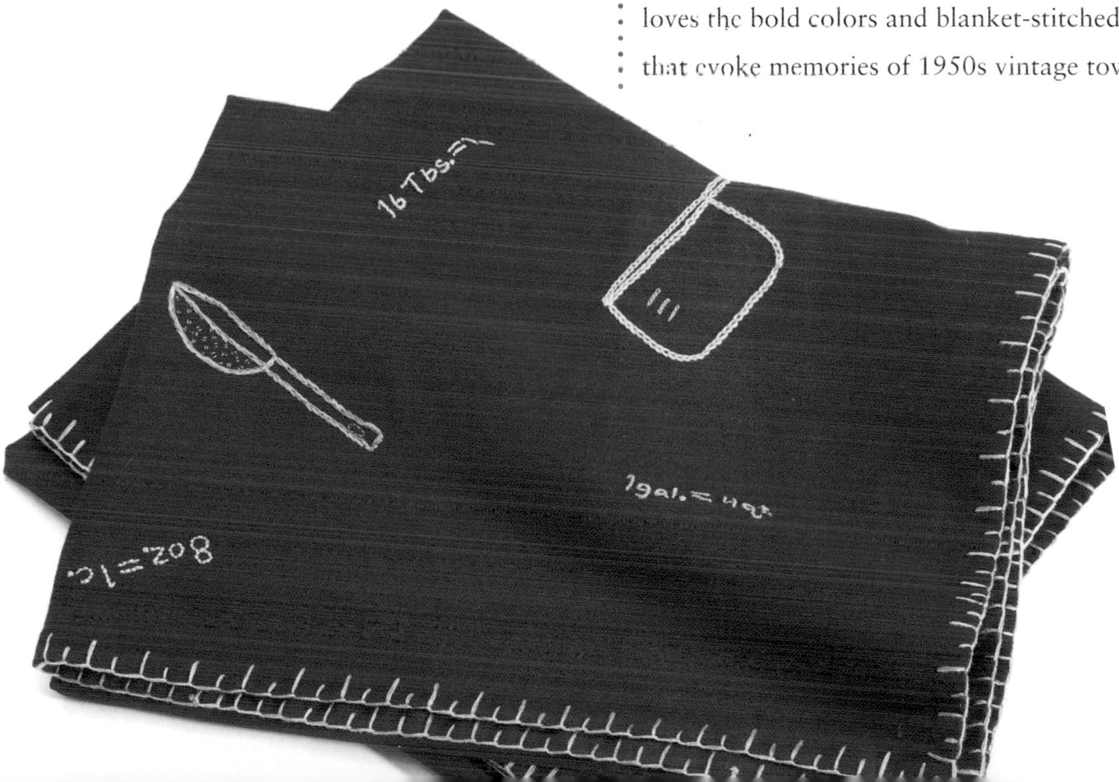

■ INSTRUCTIONS

Notes: Use the size 7 needle to work with one to two strands; use the size 9 needle to work with four strands. Refer to the patterns for color placement.

Wash and press the towels. Place the measurement conversions and measuring cups at random but make sure that the motifs are at least 1 inch (2.5 cm) from the edges of the towel. Transfer the motifs to the tea towels using one of the methods on pages 5–8. Mount one of the towels in the embroidery hoop.

■ MEASURING CUP

Use three strands of #3819 and one strand of #471 blended together to chain-stitch the bottom, sides, and lower rim line of the cup. Using chain stitch, outline the handle and upper rim line of the cup with a blend of one strand each of #3819 and #471; chain-stitch the three interior measuring lines with one strand of #3364.

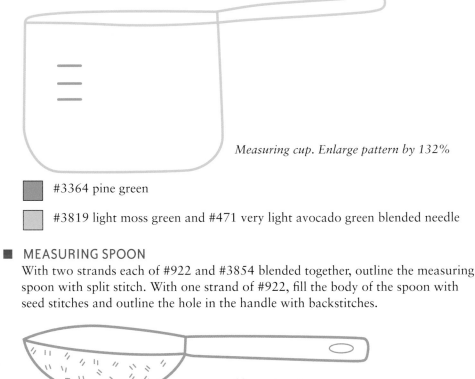

Measuring cup. Enlarge pattern by 132%

#3364 pine green

#3819 light moss green and #471 very light avocado green blended needle

■ MEASURING SPOON

With two strands each of #922 and #3854 blended together, outline the measuring spoon with split stitch. With one strand of #922, fill the body of the spoon with seed stitches and outline the hole in the handle with backstitches.

Measuring spoon

#922 light copper and #3854 medium autumn gold blended needle

#922 light copper

■ CONVERSIONS

Backstitch the letters and numbers and indicate the periods with colonial knots for the following: Use one strand each of #3819 and #471 blended together for "8 oz. = 1 c." and one strand each of #922 and #3854 blended together for "3 t. = 1 Tbs."

Use tightly whipped backstitch for the letters and numbers and indicate the periods with colonial knots for the following: Use one strand each of #3811 and #807 blended together for "16 Tbs. = 1 c.," 1 strand each of #922 and #3854 blended together for "1 gal. = 4 qt.," and 1 strand each of #471 and #3364 blended together for "16 oz. = 1 lb." Remove the towel from the hoop and repeat all the pattern transferring and stitching instructions to decorate the second towel.

8 oz. = 1c.
Ounces to cups

◻ #3819 light moss green and #471 very light avocado green blended needle

3t. = 1Tbs.
Teaspoons to tablespoons

◼ #922 light copper and #3854 medium autumn gold blended needle

16 Tbs.=1c.
Tablespoons to cups

◼ #3811 very light turquoise and #807 peacock blue blended needle

1gal.= 4qt.
Gallons to quarts

◼ #922 light copper and #3854 medium autumn gold blended needle

16oz.=1lb.
Ounces to pounds

◼ #471 very light avocado green and #3364 pine green blended needle

LONG-AND-SHORT BLANKET STITCH

Working from left to right, bring the needle up at 1 and insert at 2. Bring back up at 3 and over the working thread. Repeat by making the next stitch about twice as long as the stitch that runs from 1 to 2. Note: Regular blanket stitch is achieved by keeping the distance between 2 and 3 consistent.

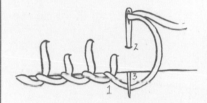

WHIPPED BACKSTITCH

Bring the needle up at the left end of a row of backstitches and wrap the working thread around one backstitch by inserting the needle from the top under the stitch—don't pierce the fabric. For loosely wrapped stitches that show the backstitches, repeat by wrapping each backstitch individually. For tightly wrapped stitches that conceal the backstitches, whip each backstitch four to five times or until covered.

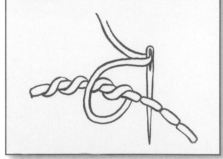

BASIC HEMS: MAKING YOUR OWN TEA TOWELS

It is easy to hem fabric to create your own tea towels with the use of one of these slip-stitch variations. The uneven slip stitch keeps your thread completely concealed in the fold of the hem, while the floats of the vertical slip-stitch are faintly visible outside the fold of the hem. Unlike a traditional slip stitch (see page 105), which results in evenly spaced, same-sized stitches, the uneven slip stitch alternates between long and short stitches. Viewing the right side of the fabric, you will see stitches perpendicular to the hem created by the vertical slip stitch and stitches parallel to the hem created by the uneven slip stitch (see Figures 1 and 2). These versatile hems can be used for everyday tasks like hemming pants.

To make a tea towel, you will need a 25- × 37-inch (63.5- × 94.0-cm) piece of 100% cotton fabric, a size 9 embroidery needle, and sewing thread to match your fabric. To prepare the fabric for hemming, fold in one side of the fabric ¼ inch (6 mm) with wrong sides facing; fold again and press. Working on the wrong side of the fabric, tack down the inside folded edge of the hem to the ground fabric with one of the following stitches:

Vertical slip stitch (Figure 3): Working from right to left, pick up a few threads of the edge of the fold. *With the needle perpendicular to the fold, pick up a few threads of the body of the towel about ¼ inch (6 mm) to the left; pick up a few threads of the edge of the fold directly below the previous stitch. Repeat from *.

Uneven slip stitch (Figure 4): Working from right to left, pick up a few threads from the body of the towel. Insert the needle into the fold of the hem about ¹⁄₁₆ inch (1.5 mm) to the left and *bring the needle out of the fold ¼ inch (6 mm) to the left; the thread will be hidden inside the fold. Repeat by picking up a few more threads from the body of the towel (see illustration) and inserting the needle into the fold again, about ¹⁄₁₆ inch (1.5 mm) to the left; repeat from *.

Hem the opposite side of the towel and then the two long sides. This method will help you achieve crisp corners.

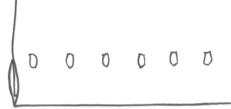

Figure 1. Vertical slip stitch (front)

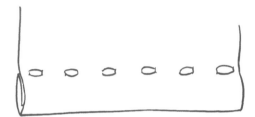

Figure 2. Uneven slip stitch (front)

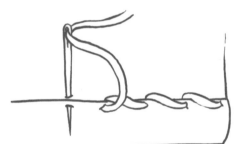

Figure 3. Vertical slip stitch (back)

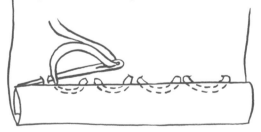

Figure 4. Uneven slip stitch (back)

■ EDGING

With three strands of #807 and one strand of #3811 blended together, decorate the hem of one towel with long-and-short blanket stitch: Work stitches ¼ inch (6 mm) apart; the long stitches are ⅜ inch (1.0 cm) in length and the short stitches are ¼ inch (6 mm) in length. On most towels, you may use the stitched hemline as a guide; adjust the stitch length as desired. Use two strands of #3819 and two strands of #471 blended together to edge the second towel with the long-and-short blanket stitch. For a smooth transition on the corners, angle the stitch that falls on the corner toward the center of the towel.

These towels keep conversions handy

CLOTHS

FOR HERBS AND FLOWERS

Why go through all the fuss of tying and hanging your flowers and herbs when you can dry them just as quickly with these pretty, open-weave drying cloths? Put them on a metal cooling rack designed for baking, and you'll be surprised how fast greenery dries. Plus, when dry, the herbs and flowers are easier to handle and pour into jars.

S P E C I F I C A T I O N S

■ SIZE

- 14½ × 12 inches
  (36.8 × 30.5 cm);
  materials given
  will make two
  cloths

■ THREADS

- 100% cotton 6-strand
  embroidery threads (I
  used DMC Embroi-
  dery Floss, Article
  117), 8.7 yards (8 m)/
  skein, 1 skein each of
  the colors listed in the
  keys; sewing thread,
  100% cotton, 1 spool
  each of purple and
  sage green

■ FABRIC

- 100% cotton: purple
  and sage green, 1 ×
  11 inches (2.5 ×
  27.9 cm), 1 piece of each
  color; Open-weave (16
  threads per inch) drapery
  fabric: purple and sage
  green, 20½ × 14 inches
  (52.1 × 35.6 cm), 1
  piece of each color

■ NOTIONS

- Nonwoven
  fusible web,
  1 × 11 inches
  (2.5 × 27.9 cm),
  4 pieces;
  needles,
  embroidery
  sizes 7 and 9
- Optional:
  sewing
  machine

■ STITCHES

- Couching, page 21
- Double running
  stitch, page 20
- French knots,
  page 21
- Lazy daisy stitch,
  page 95
- Stem stitch, page 21
- Straight stitch,
  page 20

■ INSTRUCTIONS

Note: Make sure you are using nonwoven fusible web; iron-on fabric adhesive leaves the ends of the open-weave fabric rubbery and shiny. If you are unable to find the open-weave drapery fabric with around 16 threads per inch that I used, use cheesecloth; its average thread count is 25 threads per inch. Use the size 7 needle to work with four strands of thread and the size 9 needle to work with one or two strands. Refer to the patterns for color placement.

■ ASSEMBLING THE CLOTHS

Working with one of the 20½- × 14-inch (52.1- × 35.6-cm) pieces of open-weave fabric, pull one thread 1 inch (2.5 cm) from the long side and remove by sliding the fabric down the pulled thread. Measure 12 inches (30.5 cm) from the pulled thread and remove another thread parallel to the first. Working on one of the short ends, pull and remove one thread that is 1 inch (2.5 cm) from the end, measure 18½ inch-es (47.0 cm) toward the other short end, and pull and remove another thread. Trim the edges of the short ends within ¹/₁₆ inch (1.5 mm) of the pulled threads. Repeat for the other 20½- × 14-inch (52.1- × 35.6-cm) piece of open-weave fabric.

Set the machine so that the zigzag stitches are ⅛ inch (3 mm) wide and 10 stitches per 1 inch (2.5 cm). (I set my machine's width to 3.5 and its length to 1.5; locate the dials that make these adjustments with the sewing-machine illustration on page 109.) Using the channel left by the pulled thread as a guide and thread that matches the open-weave fabric, machine stitch down one long side of the fabric with zigzag stitches, catching two threads to the inside of the channel. (The zigzag stitches will pull to the middle and not maintain the width indicated on the machine.) If you pre-fer hand stitching, whipstitch (page 103) together the two threads to the inside of the channel. Repeat on the other long side and on both long sides of the other 20½- × 14-inch (52.1- × 35.6-cm) piece of open-weave fabric.

Lay one piece of the nonwoven fusible web on top of the sage green 20½- × 14-inch (52.1- × 35.6-cm) piece of open-weave fabric with the long edge of the fusible web parallel with the short end of the open-weave fabric and centered side by side. Slide the fusible web toward the end so that the edges of the open-weave fabric and fusible web meet. (If you're working with paper-backed fusible web, fuse the web to the fabric and remove the paper.) Lay the purple 1- × 11-inch (2.5- × 27.9-cm) piece of fabric on top of the fusible web and fuse using an iron and damp press cloth according to manufacturer's directions. Fold the short end of the open-weave fabric toward the center, along the inside edge of the 1- × 11-inch (2.5- × 27.9-cm) piece of fabric and press. Fold 1 inch (2.5 cm) toward the center again and press (the raw edge of the short end is now concealed in the fold). Repeat fusing and folding instructions for the opposite end and for the purple 20½- × 14-inch (52.1-× 35.6-cm) piece of open-weave fabric, using the sage green 1- × 11-inch (2.5- × 27.9-cm) piece of fabric for the border.

■ EMBELLISHING THE CLOTHS

With the body of the sage green cloth away from you, and using one of the transfer methods on pages 5–8, transfer the Flowers pattern, on top of the sage green open-weave fabric that covers the purple strip of cotton to the end of the cloths, centered side to side, and centered between the top and bottom edge of the 1-inch (2.5-cm) folded border of the cloth. Transfer the Lavender Sprig pattern to the opposite end of the green cloth. Transfer the Herbs and Lavender Sprig patterns to the border of the purple open-weave fabric, aligning motifs as directed above. Stitch the motifs as directed below. Gently slide your fingers under the folded portion of the cloth so you do not catch the bottom body layer when you stitch—the embroidered fold will be laid down so the back of the stitches are covered.

■ FLOWERS

Couch down four strands of #3855 with two strands of #472 for the text. Make the French knots (indicated by dots) with a blended needle made of two strands each of #3803 and #3855.

 #3855 light autumn gold and #472 ultra light avocado green

#3803 dark mauve and #3855 light autumn gold blended needle

■ HERBS

Couch down four strands of #472 with two strands of #3855 for the text. Make the French knots (indicated by dots) with a blended needle made of two strands each of #472 and #3855.

▢	#472 ultra light avocado green and # 3855 light autumn gold

■ LAVENDER SPRIG

Stitch the stems and small leaves with stem stitch with a blended needle made of one strand of #3855, one strand of #472, two strands of #3011, and two strands of #3346. Make the flowers with lazy daisy stitch with a blended needle of two strands of #327 and two strands of #902. Fill the center of the lazy daisy stitches with one strand of #3855 and several small, straight stitches.

◼	#327 dark violet and #902 very dark garnet blended needle
▢	#3855 light autumn gold
◼	#3855 light autumn gold, #472 ultra light avocado green, #3011 dark khaki green, and #3346 hunter green blended needle

■ FINISHING

When you're done stitching, remove your hand to allow the back of the stitched portion to fall back down on the surface of the cloth to conceal the thread tails. Lay one of the pieces of fusible web under the stitched portion, inside the fold. With the embroidery face down on a terry-cloth towel, fuse the layers together by ironing according to manufacturer's directions. (If you're working with paper-backed fusible web, iron to fuse the web to the back of the stitches, lift up the fold to remove the paper, lay the fold back down, and iron to fuse the fold to the body of the cloth.) With thread that matches the body of the cloth, tack down the folded edge to the body of the cloth on the back: Add double running stitches along the inside edge of the fold, catching all layers of mesh fabric. Repeat finishing instructions for the opposite side and for the other cloth.

LAZY DAISY STITCH

This stitch is essentially detached chain stitch. Working from top to bottom, create a loop by bringing the needle up at 1 and reinserting at 1; do not pull the thread taut. Bring the needle up at 2 through the loop and gently pull the needle toward you so that the loop is flush to the fabric. Take a short vertical stitch to tack down the loop at 3.

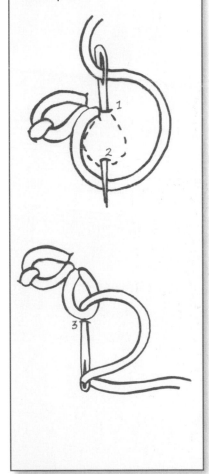

APRON

Dress up a simple apron with embroidered wine, champagne, and martini glasses and a splash of olives, and you'll be cooking and serving cocktails and hors d'oeuvres at your next party *en vogue*. For a truly unique and personalized ensemble, finish off the apron with tasteful edging. Cheers!

■ **SIZE**

31 × 29 inches (78.7 × 73.7 cm); not including strap

■ **THREADS**

100% cotton 6-strand embroidery threads (I used DMC Embroidery Floss, Article 117), 8.7 yards (8 m)/skein, 1 skein each of the colors listed in the keys; 100% pearl cotton (I used DMC No. 8, Article 116), 88 yards (80 m)/ball, one 10 g ball of #471 very light avocado green

■ **FABRIC**

Chef's apron, size and color of your choice

■ **NOTIONS**

Needles, embroidery sizes 3, 8, and 10; embroidery hoop with a fabric-wrapped inner ring, 6 inches (15.2 cm) in diameter

■ **STITCHES**

Braid edging stitch, page 98 Couching, page 21

■ **INSTRUCTIONS**

Note: Use the size 10 needle to work with single-strand couching thread and the size 3 needle to work with the multistrand couched threads. Use the size 8 needle for the edging. For tips on managing couched threads, see page 80. Refer to the patterns for color placement.

Apron sizes vary, so make adjustments as you feel necessary (I hemmed mine 2 inches [5.1 cm] so that it is 29 inches [73.7 cm] from the neckline to the bottom hem). Using one of the transfer methods on pages 5–8, transfer the glass motifs to the apron, positioning the top left corner of each glass as indicated: The champagne glass is 4½ inches (11.4 cm) from the left side and 5¾ inches (14.6 cm) from the neckline; the wine glass is 13½ inches (34.3 cm) from the bottom hem and 5 inches (12.7 cm) from the left side; the martini glass is 11¼ inches (28.6 cm) from the right side and 13 inches (33.0 cm) from the neckline. Scatter as many olives as desired randomly over the apron (I stitched twenty-two). Mount the apron in the hoop with the design to be stitched in the center, moving as necessary to work the large motifs. Remove the fabric from the hoop when stitching is complete.

You can wear this hip apron anytime

■ CHAMPAGNE GLASS

Use one strand of #3052 to couch down a blend of four strands of #3052 and one strand of #676.

■ WINE GLASS

Use one strand of #3052 to couch down a blend of four strands of #3052 and one strand of #471.

■ MARTINI GLASS

Use one strand of #3052 to couch down a blend of four strands of #3052 and one strand of #3768. Stitch the olive as directed below; stitch the toothpick by couching down five strands of #676 with one strand of thread the same color.

■ OLIVES

Couch down five strands of #471 with one strand of thread the same color. For the pimientos, couch down five strands of #676 with one strand of thread the same color.

■ GLASS NAMES (INCLUDED IN THE PATTERNS ABOVE)

Couch down three strands of #676 with one strand of thread the same color.

■ EDGING

With the #471 No. 8 thread, finish the bottom hem and neckline with braid edging stitch.

☐ #676 light old gold

▨ #3052 medium green gray and #676 light old gold blended needle

Enlarge pattern by 168%

BRAID EDGING STITCH

Working from right to left with the edge of the item to be embroidered facing away from you, bring the needle out at the edge and create a loop according to the illustration: Bring the needle through the loop from the top and insert in the fabric from the back, about ⅛ inch (3 mm) from the edge. To control the tension and size of the loop, hold the loop between two fingers while pulling the thread through the first loop and over the working thread. Repeat by taking the next stitch about ¼ inch (6 mm) to the left of the first.

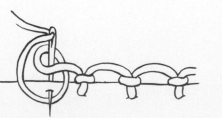

#676 light old gold

#3052 medium green gray
and #471 very light avocado
green blended needle

#471 very light avocado green

#676 light old gold

#471 very light avacado green

#676 light old gold

#3052 medium green gray and #3768
dark gray green blended needle

Enlarge patterns by 168%

WHICH CAME FIRST
NAPKIN RINGS

Which came first? That's the endless question posed by these napkin rings, and you'll love how fun they are to make because the detached buttonhole stitch offers so many three-dimensional shaping possibilities. Working with six to eight strands of thread gives quick and satisfying results, but if you're looking for a more ambitious project, try backstitching the outlines of the chicken and egg onto coordinating placemats and napkins.

■ SIZE

Egg: 2⅛ inches (5.4 cm) in diameter
Chicken: 2 × 2½ inches (5.1 × 6.4 cm)

■ THREADS

100% cotton 6-strand embroidery threads (I used DMC Embroidery Floss Article 117), 8.7 yards (8 m)/skein, 1 skein each of the colors listed in the keys; Optional: 100% rayon 6-strand embroidery threads (I used DMC Embroidery Floss, Article 1008), 8.7 yards (8 m)/skein, 1 skein each of #30762 very light pearl gray and #30745 light pale yellow

■ FABRIC

100% cotton: yellow and orange, 7 × 7 inches (17.8 × 17.8 cm), 1 piece of each color, and 3 × 3 inches (7.6 × 7.6 cm), 1 piece of each color; 100% cotton: yellow and white, scraps (about 1-inch [2.5-cm] square) for stuffing the padded areas of the napkin rings

■ NOTIONS

Medium-weight nonwoven fusible web, 3 × 3 inches (7.6 × 7.6 cm) square, 2 pieces; needles, tapestry size 22 and embroidery size 9; embroidery hoop, 6 inches (15.2 cm) in diameter; ribbon, 100% silk, ⅛ inch (4 mm) wide, cream, 5 inches (12.7 cm) long, 4 pieces; napkin rings, ¼ inch (6mm) wide, 2

■ STITCHES

Backstitch, page 20
Colonial knot, page 35
Double running stitch, page 20
Whipstitch, page 103
Detached buttonhole stitch, page 102

■ INSTRUCTIONS

Note: Use the size 9 embroidery needle when working with two strands of thread; use the size 22 tapestry needle when working with more than two strands. Refer to the patterns for color placement.

Using one of the transfer methods on pages 5–8, transfer the egg pattern to the 7-inch (17.8-cm) yellow square of fabric and the chicken pattern (page 103) to the 7-inch (17.8-cm) orange square of fabric. To cover areas with detached buttonhole stitch and the tapestry needle as directed below, use the row of backstitches (indicated by dashed lines) as the foundation for the first row of netting and work in the direction indicated by the arrows on the pattern. Keep the stitches within the solid and dashed lines, filling each shape individually. Feel free to experiment with color and the number of strands when you're mixing the blended needles; a slight shift in color gives the shapes more dimension and helps conserve thread by using up leftover single strands.

■ EGG

Mount the 7-inch (17.8-cm) yellow square piece of fabric in the hoop and stitch the dashed lines of the pattern in backstitch with two strands of blanc. Work the egg-white area in detached buttonhole stitch with a blend of two strands of blanc, two strands of ecru, one strand of #613, and one strand of #739; for shine, replace one of the strands of blanc with one strand of #30762. For the yolk, use detached buttonhole stitch and a blend of two strands of #742, three strands of #743, and one strand of #745; for shine, replace #745 with #30745. Increase the number of stitches as you near the center of the yolk to allow space for the stuffing. When the yolk shape is three-quarters complete, insert the scraps of yellow fabric to create the three-dimensional yolk. Decrease the stitches as you complete the yellow center, inserting a few more of the yellow fabric scraps just before closing. If desired, pad one or two sections of the border with the white scraps of fabric to give the egg more dimension. Remove the fabric from the hoop.

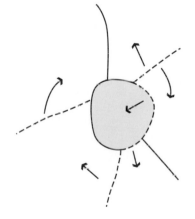

blanc, ecru, #613 very light drab brown, #739 ultra very light tan, #30762 very light pearl gray (optional) blended needle

#742 light tangerine, #743 medium yellow, #745 light pale yellow, and #30745 rayon light pale yellow (optional) blended needle

Egg pattern

DETACHED BUTTONHOLE STITCH AND SHAPING TECHNIQUES

Begin by stitching a row of foundation stitches with backstitch or double running stitch (see Figure 1). Bring the needle up at the left side of the foundation row (1), about ⅛ to 1/16 inch (3 cm to 1.5 mm) below the first stitch. Working from left to right, and referring to Figure 1, pull the needle under one stitch in the foundation row and over the loop created by the working thread; pull taut. Repeat and complete the row by making one loop in each stitch of the foundation row.

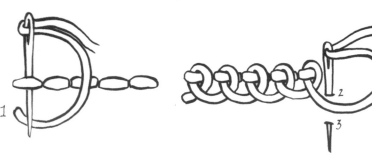

Figure 1. Foundation row

Figure 2. Row change

When the row is complete, insert the needle into the fabric (2) and bring up ⅛ to 1/16 inch (3 cm to 1.5 mm) below the last stitch (3), referring to Figure 2. Work from right to left (mirroring the stitch motion used when moving from left to right) into the loops created in the previous row, referring to Figure 3. The interlocked stitches will create a netlike web on the surface of the fabric.

Figure 3. Working the second row

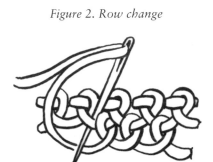

Figure 4. Increasing

To increase the number of stitches, take more than one stitch into the loops of the previous row—you will create a three-dimensional surface that allows space for padding. For subtle increases, take two stitches with the working thread into one loop of the previous row in the middle of the shape to be filled (see Figure 4) before moving to the next stitch.

To either close up a three-dimensional area or narrow a design element, simply decrease the number of stitches by skipping a stitch (doing so will not alter the integrity of the web). To avoid holes, do not skip two stitches adjacent to each other. If I accidentally create holes, I fill them with small French knots or simply loop the working thread around an adjacent stitch with the same color thread.

Figure 5. Closing a shape

When you're completing an area, tack down each loop from the last row of stitches to secure to the ground fabric and complete the shape (see Figure 5).

CHICKEN

Mount the 7-inch (17.8-cm) orange square piece of fabric in the hoop and stitch the dashed lines of the pattern in backstitch with two strands of blanc. Using detached buttonhole stitch, stitch the body of the chicken with a blended needle made of two strands of blanc, one strand of #712, and two strands of #739; a blend of two strands of #613, two strands of #712, one strand of #921, and one strand of #738 for the wing; a blend of two strands of #743 and two strands of #3855 for the beak; and a blend of one strand of #150 and three strands of #815 for the comb. Use three strands of #3371 to make a colonial knot for the eye. Increase the number of stitches on the wing and pad with the white fabric scraps; decrease the stitches as you complete the wing, inserting a few more white fabric scraps just before closing. Remove the fabric from the hoop.

FINISHING

Trim the fabric within ½ inch (1.3 cm) of the outlines. For the tight curves of the chicken, you will need to cut notches (small Vs cut in the fabric toward the stitching) in the fabric around the curved areas; notches should be at least ¹⁄₁₆ inch (1.5 mm) away from the stitches. Fold the raw edges of the fabric to the back and whipstitch to the back with the embroidery needle and one strand of blanc thread. If needed, make a few stitches close to the edge to pull back the fabric—you want some of the stitched edge to curl to the back.

Fuse one piece of fusible web to the 3-inch (7.6-cm) yellow square piece of fabric. With the paper side facing up, center the egg right-side up on the square and trace around the shape. Cut out the shape, trimming just inside the drawn line; peel off the paper and fuse to the back of the stitching. To secure the fabrics together, whipstitch around the edge of the backing fabric with matching thread. Fuse the other fusible web square to the orange piece of fabric. Follow the techniques above to adhere the orange backing piece of fabric to the chicken.

To attach the egg to the napkin ring, thread the tapestry needle with a 5-inch (12.7-cm) piece of silk ribbon and take a small (¼-inch [6-mm]) long stitch into the backing, ¼ inch (6 mm) left of center; pull the ribbon halfway through. Insert another ribbon ¼ inch (6 mm) to the right of center. Tie the egg to the napkin ring, double knot, and trim the ribbon tails to ¼ inch (6 mm). Attach two ribbons to the back of the chicken in the same manner and tie to the second napkin ring.

Chicken pattern

blanc, #712 cream, and #739 ultra very light tan blended needle

#613 very light drab brown, #712 cream, #921 copper, and #738 very light tan blended needle

#743 medium yellow and #3855 light autumn gold blended needle

#150 ultra very dark dusty rose and #815 medium garnet blended needle

#3371 black brown

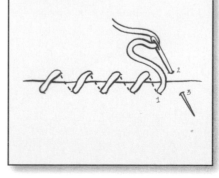

WHIPSTITCH
Bring the needle up at 1, insert at 2, and bring up at 3. These quick stitches do not have to be very tight or close together.

HYBRID GRID
PILLOWS

These nifty pillows are hybrids—they combine both machine- and hand-stitched motifs, so they're an ideal project for beginners. The grid pattern for the red machine-embroidered pillow is similar to a sewing exercise I was assigned in my first textile class, so you know it's not too complicated to craft. The featured stitch for this project, the slip stitch, is easy, versatile, and practical for everyday use.

■ SIZE	■ THREADS	■ FABRIC	■ NOTIONS	■ STITCHES
Red: 15 × 15 inches (38.1 × 38.1 cm) Green: 10 × 10 inches (25.4 × 25.4 cm)	100% cotton embroidery threads (I used DMC Pearl Cotton No. 8 Article 116), 88 yards (80 m)/ball, one 10 g ball each of #815 medium garnet and #920 medium copper; sewing thread, 100% cotton, lime green, purple, red, and green	100% cotton: red, 10¼ × 10¼ inches (26.0 × 26.0 cm), 1 piece and 11 × 11 inches (27.9 × 27.9 cm), 1 piece; 100% cotton: green, 12 × 12 inches (30.5 × 30.5 cm), 1 piece and 16 × 16 inches (40.6 × 40.6 cm 1 piece); 100% cotton: purple, 2½ × 15 inches (6.4 × 38.1 cm), 4 pieces; 100% cotton: yellow, 5½ × 17 inches (14.0 × 43.2 cm), 4 pieces	Medium-weight nonwoven fusible interfacing, 9¼ × 9¼ inches (23.5 × 23.5 cm) 1 piece; 7¼ × 7¼ inches (18.4 × 18.4 cm) 1 piece; 1½ × 10½ inches (3.8 × 26.7 cm) 4 pieces, and 4½ × 15 inches (11.4 × 38.1 cm), 4 pieces; needles, embroidery sizes 6 and 8; embroidery hoop, 6 inches (15.2 cm) in diameter; fabric-marking pen or pencil; fine-point permanent marker, green or other mid-range color; fiberfill, 16 oz (453.6 g) bag; pins; sewing machine	Running stitch, page 20 Slip stitch, below

■ HAND EMBROIDERY FOR THE GREEN PILLOW

Using the interfacing transfer method (page 7), transfer Pattern 1 (page 107) for the body of the green pillow to the 12-inch (30.5-cm) square of green fabric: Tape the pattern to a flat surface; center and tape the 7¼-inch (18.4-cm) square piece of interfacing on top of the pattern; trace the pattern onto the interfacing with the permanent marker. Remove the tape. Center and fuse the interfacing to the wrong side of the 12-inch (30.5-cm) square of green fabric, according to manufacturer's directions.

Mount the fabric in the hoop with interfacing right-side up. With a size 8 needle and #815, use running stitches to complete the pattern, making sure to keep the knots on the side with the interfacing. Remove the fabric from the hoop and press right-side down on a terry-cloth towel. With the embroidery centered, trim the fabric to measure 8¼-inches (21.0-cm) square.

To make the purple border, transfer Pattern 2 (page 108) with the interfacing transfer method, as directed above, to one of the 1½- × 10½-inch (3.8- × 26.7-cm) pieces of interfacing; center and fuse the pattern to one of the 2½- × 15-inch (6.4- × 38.1-cm) strips of purple fabric. Mount the fabric in the hoop with the interfacing right-side up. With the size 6 needle, stitch the pattern with #920, keeping the knots on the side with the interfacing. Remove the fabric from the hoop and press right-side down on a terry-cloth towel. With the embroidery centered, trim the fabric to measure 2½ × 11 inches (6.4 × 27.9 cm). Repeat for the three remaining sides.

SLIP STITCH

Working from right to left, join two pieces of fabric by taking a ¼-inch (6 mm) long stitch into the folded edge of one piece of fabric and bringing the needle out. Insert the needle into the folded edge of the other piece of fabric, directly across from the point where the thread emerged from the previous stitch. Repeat by inserting the needle into the first piece of fabric. The thread will be almost entirely hidden inside the folds of the fabrics.

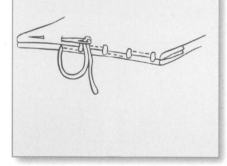

■ MACHINE EMBROIDERY FOR THE RED PILLOW

Center and fuse the 9¼-inch (23.5-cm) square piece of interfacing to the back of the 10¼-inch (26.0-cm) square piece of red fabric. With a ruler and the fabric-marking pen or pencil, draw a cross in the center of the interfacing; lines should be parallel to the edges and extend across the width of the fabric. With a sewing machine, lime green thread, and the interfacing right side up, stitch from one fabric edge to the other along one of the lines. Align the side of the presser foot with the stitched line (the needle should be about ¼ inch [6 mm] from the previous line) and sew another line across the fabric. Continue to use the side of the presser foot as your guide and cover the fabric with parallel lines. Complete the grid with the same method, using the other line of the drawn cross that is perpendicular to the previous stitched lines as your guide for the initial line. There is no need to back tack (reverse stitches that secure the beginning and end of a stitched line) at the start and finish of each line because the lines will be sewn over. Trim the thread tails. For visual texture, see the swatches with variegated sewing threads, below.

To make the yellow border, use the interfacing transfer method as directed above to transfer Pattern 3 (page 108) to one of the four 4 ½- × 15-inch (11.4- × 38.1-cm) pieces of interfacing: Repeat pattern so that five evenly spaced rows completely cover the length of the interfacing (Pattern 3). Center and fuse the pattern to one of the 5½- × 17-inch (14.0- × 43.2-cm) strips of yellow fabric. Machine stitch with the purple thread by starting on the outside line of one of the squares and working toward the center; keep the needle in the fabric to make the 90-degree turns. Use the side of the presser foot as a guide to keep uniform space between the lines. Press right-side down on a terry-cloth towel. With the design centered, trim to 4 × 16 inches (10.2 × 40.6 cm). Repeat for the three remaining sides.

■ PILLOW CONSTRUCTION

To construct one pillow, align and center one raw edge of the border with one edge of the body piece, right sides facing. Machine stitch (or hand stitch with tightly spaced double running or backstitches) together with ½-inch (1.3-cm) seam allowance, stopping and starting ½ inch (1.3 cm) from the sides of the body piece. Repeat on the three remaining sides.

To construct the mitered corner, fold the body diagonally in half and align the long sides of the border pieces, with right-sides facing. Lay the ruler on the fabric with the edge aligned with the diagonal fold and extend the line created by the ruler with the marking pen across the border pieces. Carefully lift the ruler and pin the stacked border pieces together. Fold the seam allowances of the border and

Try variegated sewing threads

Pattern 1. Enlarge pattern by 174%   ■ #815 medium garnet

body toward the center of the pillow. Starting at the raw edges of the border pieces, machine stitch (or hand stitch with tightly spaced double running or backstitches) along the drawn line, stopping at the point where the seam joins the border and the body. Repeat along the drawn line on the other side of the diagonal fold. Trim the fabric within ½ inch (1.3 cm) of the new seam and press the seam open. Refold the fabric diagonally in half in the other direction, draw another diagonal line, and join the borders to finish the two remaining corners as directed above; unfold.

Press the seam allowances of the border and body away from the center. With right sides facing, center and pin the embroidered front of the pillow on top of the backing piece. The red backing fabric for the green pillow is 11 inches (27.9 cm) square; the green backing fabric for the red pillow is 16 inches (40.6 cm) square. Join the pieces by machine stitching (or hand stitching with tightly spaced double running or backstitches) ½ inch (1.3 cm) from the raw edges of the border piece; stitch all four sides but leave a 5-inch (12.7-cm) opening on one side. Clip the corners and trim the seam allowances to ¼ inch (6 mm). Turn right-sides out, push the corners out with a knitting needle or chopstick, and press.

To make the flange border and offset the body from the border, insert pins around the perimeter of the body piece on the inside of the seam that joins the body to the border. Join the pillow front to the backing fabric with a running stitch, size 6 needle, and sewing thread that matches the body fabric (red or green); leave a 5-inch (12.7-cm) opening on one side that aligns with the opening in the outside seam. Remove pins and insert fiberfill through both openings. Enclose the stuffing by pinning through all layers of fabric with the pins to the inside of the seam that joins the body fabric to the border. Complete the running stitches to close the inside 5-inch (12.7-cm) opening. To close the outside opening, fold the raw edges of the border and backing fabric toward the center of the pillow ½ inch (1.3 cm), press, pin, and slip-stitch closed.

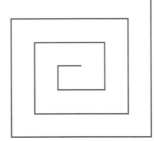 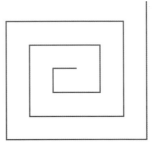

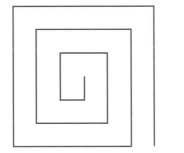 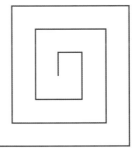

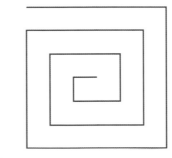 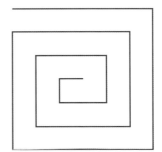

■ #920 medium copper

Pattern 2. Enlarge pattern by 133%

■ Purple sewing thread

Pattern 3. Enlarge pattern by 128%

SEWING MACHINE BASICS

· A well-cared-for machine will last for years; keep your machine oiled, lint-free, and the tension balanced (page 77). It is well worth the expense to take your machine to a sewing-machine repair shop for regular tune-ups.

· Change your needles often; dull needles make the machine work harder, are easy to break, and may distort fabric by pulling threads. Dull and bent needles make stitches uneven; bent needles can chip a machine's needle plate.

· Make sure to use the appropriate needle size for the fabric and thread you are working with, as well as the size recommended by your machine's manufacturer. As a general rule for working with woven fabrics, a size 80 needle is the most versatile (good for cotton and medium-weight fabrics); size

100 is best for heavyweight fabrics like canvas, denim, and upholstery; size 65 is good for silk. Use a ballpoint (or "stretch") needle for sewing knitted fabrics; use a size 70 for jersey, nylon, and lightweight fabrics, a size 80 for T-shirts, and a size 90 for heavier knits like sweatshirts. Universal needles will work for both woven and knit fabrics and are available in sizes 60 to 110.

· Match the fiber content of your fabric with your thread to ensure that the fibers wear evenly. Unmatched fiber content may cause puckering and distortion during washing. Unless you're working with decorative threads, the fiber content of your top and bottom thread should always match.

· Keep thick and decorative threads in your bobbin. Doing so prevents the thread from having to travel through the needle. Remember to stitch with the wrong side of the fabric face up.

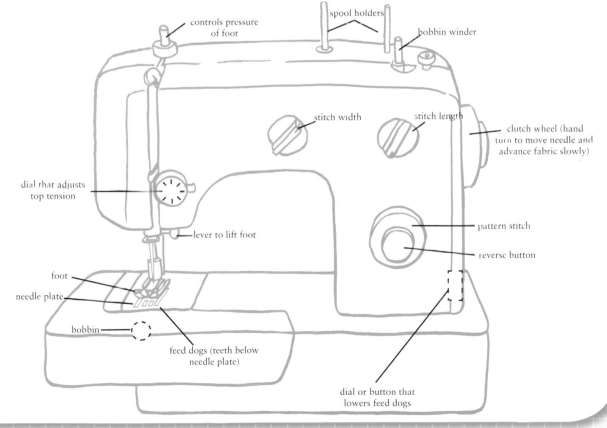

controls pressure of foot

spool holders

bobbin winder

stitch width

stitch length

clutch wheel (hand turn to move needle and advance fabric slowly)

dial that adjusts top tension

lever to lift foot

pattern stitch

reverse button

foot

needle plate

bobbin

feed dogs (teeth below needle plate)

dial or button that lowers feed dogs

ALL-MINE MONOGRAMMED
CASES

Embroider initials on these cases to make them one-of-a-kind; anyone will enjoy their organizational help. The size of these versatile cases may be easily altered to accommodate almost any storable objects. I made the large case for storing crochet hooks and knitting needles, although it could also be used for paintbrushes or silverware. The small case is suitable for pens, pencils, manicure tools, cosmetics, threads, and jewelry.

SPECIFICATIONS

■ SIZE

Large case:
10 × 10½ inches
(25.4 × 26.7 cm)

Small case:
5¾ × 10½ inches
(14.6 × 26.7 cm)

■ THREADS

100% cotton 6-strand embroidery threads (I used DMC Embroidery, Floss Article 117), 8.7 yards (8 m)/skein, 1 skein each of #221 very dark shell pink, #902 very dark garnet, #3011 dark khaki green, and #3013 light khaki green or 2 colors of your choice to coordinate with the patterned fabrics and contrast with the solid fabrics

■ FABRIC

For the small case: 100% cotton, 2 coordinating patterns, 7¼ × 11¾ inches (18.4 × 29.9 cm) for the outside, 1 piece, and 11¾ × 10 inches (29.9 × 25.4 cm) for the lining, 1 piece. One solid color: 13 × 6 inches (33.0 × 15.2 cm) for the monogram background, 1 piece; For the large case: 100% cotton, 2 coordinating prints, 18½ × 11¾ inches (47.0 × 29.9 cm) for the outside, 1 piece each, and 11¾ × 15¾ inches (29.9 × 40.0 cm) for the lining, 1 piece. One solid color: 13 × 6 inches (33.0 × 15.2 cm) for the monogram background, 1 piece; Muslin: 100% cotton, white, 10 × 11¾ inches (25.4 × 29.9 cm) for the small case; 15¾ × 11¾ inches (40.0 × 29.9 cm) for the large case; 1 piece for each case if using light-color fabric for the lining

■ NOTIONS

Lightweight nonwoven fusible web, 10 × 11¾ inches (25.4 × 29.9 cm) for the small case, 15¾ × 11¾ inches (40.0 × 29.9 cm) for the large case, 1 piece for each case if using light-colored fabric for the lining; grosgrain ribbon, ½ inch (1.3 cm) wide, 26 inches (66.0 cm) long, 2 pieces of light green and 1 piece of sage green; embroidery hoop, 5 inch (12.7 cm) in diameter; needle, embroidery size 9; fabric-marking pen or pencil; Optional: sewing machine

■ STITCHES

Backstitch, page 20

Double running stitch, page 20

Padded satin stitch over backstitch, page 112

Satin stitch, page 20

Slip stitch, page 105

Stem stitch, page 21

■ INSTRUCTIONS

Note: Use a ½-inch (2.5-cm) seam allowance for all seams. If you choose to hand stitch the seams, use tightly spaced double running stitches.

Using one of the transfer methods on pages 5–8, transfer the monograms to the upper right-hand corner of the 6- × 13-inch (15.2- × 33.0-cm) piece of fabric (the edges of the monogram should be about 2 inches [5.1 cm] from the top and right edges of the fabric). You may either stem stitch or backstitch the thin lines of the letters. (I used stem stitch for the K and backstitch for the B.) Outline the wide areas in either stem stitch or backstitch and satin-stitch the area to be filled, covering the outlines. For a more casual look, use a blended needle; I used one strand each of #221 and #902 for the K and one strand each of #3011 and #3013 for the B.

Find the center of the monogram and mark a horizontal line 1¾ inch (4.5 cm) above the letter and a vertical line 2¼ inches (5.7 cm) to the right side of the letter. With a ruler, extend these lines across the fabric with the marking pen or pencil;

PADDED SATIN STITCH OVER BACKSTITCH

Outline the shape with backstitch and fill the wide areas with rows of backstitch according to the illustration. Cover the backstitches with satin stitch; bring the needle up at 1, insert at 2, and bring up at 3. To combine satin-stitched shapes with lines of backstitch, narrow the satin stitches at the end of the shape to create a smooth transition and, if necessary, angle the satin stitches to cover the first backstitches of the lines.

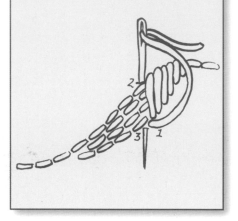

trim fabric along the lines. Trim the two remaining edges so that the piece measures 3¾ × 11¾ inches (9.5 × 29.9 cm). For the small case, machine or hand stitch a 7¼- × 11¾-inches (18.4- × 29.9-cm) piece of fabric to the bottom edge of the monogrammed piece with right sides facing and the long sides aligned. For the large case, trim and stitch to the monogrammed piece the 15¾- × 11¾-inch (40.0- × 29.9-cm) piece of fabric in the same manner. Press the seams open and set aside.

If you're working with a light-colored lining fabric, fuse the 10- × 11¾-inch (25.4- × 29.9-cm) piece of muslin fabric to the wrong side of the 10- × 11¾-inch (25.4- × 29.9-cm) lining piece with the same size piece of fusible web; doing so adds stability and prevents darker fabric from showing through lighter lining fabrics. For the large case, repeat fusing, using the 18½- × 11¾-inch (47.0- × 29.9-cm) pieces of fusible web, muslin, and lining fabric.

Lay the two previously seamed pieces on the coordinating size of lining fabric with right sides facing. Machine or hand stitch together around all edges, leaving a 6-inch (15.2-cm) opening in one of the seams; trim seam allowances to ¼ inch (6 mm) and trim the corners close to the seam allowances. Turn right sides out and press. To achieve crisp corners, use a knitting needle or chopstick to push the corners out. Fold in the remaining raw edges of the opening ½ inch (1.3 cm), press, and close the opening with slip stitch.

With the monogram face down, fold up the bottom edge (with the lining fabric facing) so that it is 2¾ inches (7.0 cm) from the top edge. Pin and baste three vertical lines on the case and slip-stitch the side seams together.

Make pockets by machine or hand stitching vertical lines across the lower half of the case spaced appropriately for its final use. For manicure tools and cosmetics, I measured from the left, marking vertical lines with the marking pen or pencil that extend across the bottom flap at 1¼, 2½, 3¾, 5, 6¼, 7½, 8½, and 9¾ inches (3.2, 6.4, 9.5, 12.7, 15.9, 19.1, 21.6, and 24.8 cm). For the large case, I made the lines of the middle panel about ¾ inch (1.9 cm) apart to accommodate small crochet hooks and knitting needles. To indicate the folds, you must have lines at 3¾ and 7½ inches (9.5 and 19.1 cm) when you're adjusting the lines for your own case.

Join the layers by machine or hand stitching along the drawn lines, temporarily omitting the lines at 3¾ and 7½ inches (9.5 and 19.1 cm). If you're machine stitching the lines, do not back tack (quick reverse stitches that secure the beginning and end of the sewn line). Instead, pull the bobbin thread to the front and knot twice with the top thread. Thread the embroidery needle with the tails and hide them by taking a 1-inch (2.5-cm) long stitch under the fabric along the seam and pulling to the front. Trim the thread tails where they emerge from the fabric.

With the interior of the case face down, center and pin the ribbon over the horizontal seam that runs below the monogram. For the large case, place the bottom edge of the second ribbon 2½ inches (6.4 cm) above the bottom edge. Stitch the vertical fold lines previously omitted to secure the ribbon and create the inside pockets. With the case lining-side down, lay the right end of the ribbon over the right-most fold with the monogram; use double running stitches to secure the ribbon to the seam that joins the front to the lining. Turn the case over and fold the case in thirds, starting by folding the right side to the center; tie the ribbons together to close the case. To adjust the overall size of the cases, alter the height of the printed fabrics and, if applicable, the muslin.

What can you store in these cases?

DESIGNING YOUR OWN FONT SUITABLE FOR MONOGRAMS

Standard software programs often offer just a few script fonts to choose from, and most are unsuitable for monograms. To solve this problem, I like to alter letters to create my own fonts. Exaggerate the wide and narrow lines of the letters and, if desired, add scrolls and knots to dress them up. Here I took Batang italics (top), added scrolls, and exaggerated the thick lines.

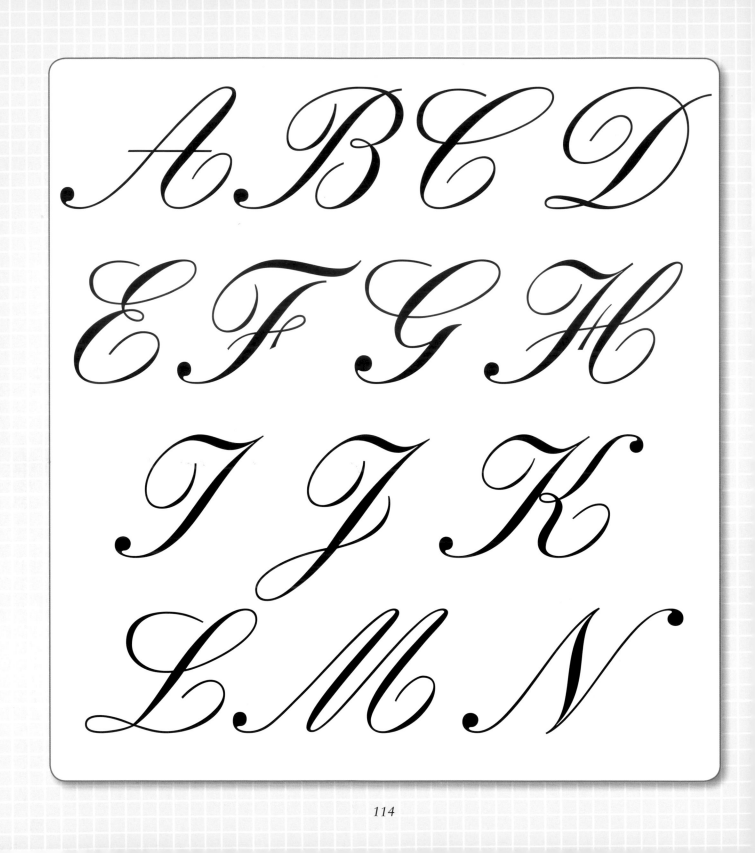

SUPPLIERS

Visit your local or online needlework stores for the products used in this book. If you are unable to locate a store in your area, contact the companies directly.

The Caron Collection
55 Old South Ave.
Stratford, CT 06615
(203) 381-9999
www.caron-net.com; mail@caron-net.com

Coats and Clark
PO Box 12229
Greenville, SC 29612-0229
(800) 648-1479
www.coatsandclark.com

DMC Corporation
South Hackensack Ave.
Port Kearny Bldg. 10 F
South Kearny, NJ 07032
www.dmc.com; dmcusa@dmc.fr

Kolo, LLC
PO Box 572
Windsor, CT 06095-0572
(888) 636-5656
www.kolo.com

Pearsall's Embroidery Silk
Tristan Brooks Designs
182 Green Glade Rd.
Memphis, TN 38120-2218
(901) 767-8414
www.tristanbrooks.com; info@tristanbrooks.com

YLI Corporation
161 West Main St.
Rock Hill, SC 29730
(803) 985-3100
www.ylicorp.com; ylicorp@ylicorp.com

INDUSTRY RESOURCES

Use the contact information below to locate a shop, refine or learn a new technique, join a guild, or learn about the needlework industry and community.

ANG
American Needlepoint Guild, Inc.
PO Box 1027
Cordova, TN 38088-1027
www.needlepoint.org; membership@needlepoint.org

EGA
Embroiderer's Guild of America, Inc.
335 West Broadway, Ste. 100
Louisville, KY 40202-2105
(502) 589-6956
www.egausa.org; egahq@egausa.org

TNNA
The National NeedleArts Association
PO Box 3388
Zanesville, OH 43702-3388
(740) 455-6773
www.tnna.org; tnna.info@offinger.com

INDEX

Anchor 3, 5

backstitch 20
  padded satin stitch over 112
  whipped 89
  with beads 57
bead embroidery 56
blanket stitch, long-and-short 89
bobbins, wrapping 12
bookbinding stitch 19
braid stitch edging 98
buttonhole stitch 71
  detached 102

canvas, mesh transfer 7
carbon, dressmaker's 7
chain stitch 21
coral stitch 84
couched threads 80
couching 21
  with beads 57
cutting mats 3
cutters 3

design, font 113
  map 85
double running stitch 20
DMC 3, 5

edging, braid stitch 98
  knot stitch 41
embroidery frames 8, 9
  hoops 8, 9

fabric, backs 31
  cutting 3
  stamping 62

iron transfers and printing on 67
fabrics, choosing 2
  preparation 2
fern stitch, one-sided 63
frames, embroidery 8, 9
French knots 21
fusible web 4, 5

hems, basic 90
herringbone stitch 57
hoops, wrapping 9

interfacing, fusible 4, 7, 8

knot stitch edging 41
knots, Colonial 35
  hiding 27

lattice pattern filling stitch 47
laundering, see washing
lazy daisy stitch 95
long-and-short satin stitch 20

monograms 114–115
  designing fonts for 113

needle pullers 9
needles 10–11

overcast stitch 21

paper, tissue 8
patterns, transferring 5–7, 8
pencils, fabric-marking 6
pens, fabric-marking 5–6
pockets, how to sew 42
projects: Apron 96–99

Baby Bib 58–63
Bag 64–66, 68–69
Butterfly Picture Frame 70–73
Cases 110–115
Cloths for Herbs and Flowers 92–95
Corduroy Coat 28, 29
Crewel Mittens 44–45, 47
Gift Tags, Cards, and Notebooks 74–77
Guitar Pick Case 78–79, 81
Hair Ties 32–35, 37
Hair-Tie Tote 36
Map Photo Album 82–85
Napkin Rings 100–101, 103
Pillows 104–108
Stitch Reference and Needle-Storage Book 16–18, 19
Textile Scrapbook 38–43
Thimbles 22–26
Towels 86–91
Velvet Ribbons and Beaded Bag 49–55

quilting basics 68–69

resources 116
ribbons, reversible 53
running stitch 20

satin stitch 20, 31
    bound 81
    over double running stitch 30
    padded 112
scissors 4
seed stitch 20
sewing machine, basics 109
    tension 77
silk, working with 73
slip stitch 90, 105
split stitch 21
stem stitch 21
straight stitch 20
stitches 20–21
    back of fabric 31
    backstitch with beads 57
    bookbinding 19

bound satin 81
braid edging 98
buttonhole 71
choosing 30, 31
coral 84
couching with beads 57
detached buttonhole 102
herringbone 57
knot stitch edging 41
lattice pattern filling 47
lazy daisy 95
long-and-short blanket 89
modified surface satin 31
one-sided fern 63
padded satin over backstitch 112
satin over double running 30
slip 90, 105
surface satin 31
whip 103
whipped backstitch 89
whipped stem 24
suppliers 116

tailor's chalk 6
tension, sewing machine 77
thimbles 9
thread conditioner 12, 13
    conversion chart 15
thread tails, hiding 27
threads, beginning 14
    choosing 2
    couched 80
    ending 14
    preparation 2
    organizing 12
    separating 13
    wool 46
Tips and techniques: avoiding bulk on the underside of
    fabric 31
    backing embroideries: making reversible ribbons 53
    basic hems 90
    bead embroidery 56
    choosing durable stitches 30

    designing an embroidered map 85

    detached buttonhole stitch and shaping 102

    hiding knots and thread tails 27

    how to bind a book 19

    how to sew a pocket 42

    tips for iron transfers and printing on fabric 67

    understanding and using sewing machine tension 77

    sewing machine basics 109

    working with silk and wire 73

    working with wool threads 46

tools 14

transfers, iron 67

transferring methods 5–7, 8

washing 2

whipped stitch 24

whipstitch 103

wire, working with 73

KNIT A BACK-TO-SCHOOL CAP, TAPESTRY CROCHET A CAT PILLOW

Needlework's Living Legacy

Embroidered
CHINESE TIGER SHOES

Appliqué an
EASY BUTTERFLY

Elegant
MONOGRAMS

PIECEWORK.

In each issue of *PieceWork* you'll be treated to examples of **beautiful needlework**. You'll learn the **history of the techniques** and the people behind the needlework, and you'll find **lots of projects**. We've added a new column (**Findings**—using, reusing, new, old, or found textiles) and reprised a reader-favorite column from the past (**Trimmings**—a sampling of patterns and charts for you to use any way you like); incorporated projects for all skill levels, each **a contemporary take on tradition**.

$21.00/year (6 issues)
Subscribe online at www.interweave.com or call 1-800-340-7496
Dept: AHTS5

An *Essential* Tool for *Every* Needleworker!

The Needleworker's Companion
Shay Pendray

An essential tool for all stitchers, authored by one of the craft's most popular and visible icons. This pocket-sized, spiral-bound reference guide is designed to fit in your needlework bag or basket. Overflowing with useful information for any stitcher: fabric counts, needle sizes, suitable threads, frames and hoops, starting and ending threads, cross-stitch, whitework, blackwork, stumpwork, ribbon embroidery, canvas work, and stitch diagrams. Filled with illustrations, this step-by-step technique book is a must-have for every stitcher.

$19.95, Spiral-bound, 7 × 5, 112 pages, ISBN 1-931499-07-1

PIECEWORK MAGAZINE PRESENT

THE

NEEDLEWORKER'S
COMPANION